Rowdy Kids

Guide to

Multiplication

Written by: Chris and Jenny Kjorness

Cogi Garden Educational Resources

Cogi Garden Books

ISBN: 0692837701
ISBN-13: 978- 0692837702

Hi there, rowdy kid!

Welcome to the *Rowdy Kids Guide to Multiplication*!

We set up this multiplication book in short-ish daily workouts so that you can build your skills every day and have **FUN** doing it.

ALSO, we tried to write the questions about things that you care about—like ice cream, hamsters, and water slides (seriously, who doesn't like water slides?!)

Sometimes we just went for funny or ridiculous. (Who knows? It *might* be important to be able to figure out how many marshmallows it would take to cover your entire bedroom floor. Right?)

Every minute that you work in this workbook you will be building skills that will allow you to do cool stuff, make awesome things, and solve important problems. And it will be fun!

So, get to it! Try hard! And if you run into something tricky, just remember the rowdy kids way:

Work Hard and Have Fun Doing It!

Let's get rowdy, Math Star!

Day 1

Lets Learn Something!

OK- multiplication is really just a shortcut to adding the same number over and over.

Say you're at the pet store and you're trying to get your parents to buy hamsters for you and your best friends. There are five of you. You need to have enough hamsters so that every one of the 5 kids in your group has 2 hamsters each (you wouldn't the hamsters to be lonely would you?) How many hamsters do you need?

To solve this you would need to add two five times:

2+2+2+2+2 = 10

An easier way to write this is:

5 X 2 = 10

(5 times of adding 2)

Now you can solve any multiplication problem!

Cool Fact: When you multiply, the numbers being multiplied are called ***factors*** and the number that is the answer is called the ***product.***

In 5 X 2 = 10, 5 and 2 are the **factors** and 10 is the **product**.

Work It Out!

Turn these multiplication problems into repeated addition. Like a Boss!

2 X 3 = ? 3+3 = 6	3 X 6 = ? 6+6+6=18	2 X 9 = 9+9=18
3 X 12 = 12+12+12=36	2 X 5 = 5+5=10	3 X 2 = 3+3=6
3 X 3 = 3+3+3=9	1 X 11 = 11	3 X 4 = 4+4+4=12
2 X 7 = 7+7=14	1 X 8 = 8	3 X 10 = 10+10+10=30

Build Your Skill!

Skip counting is counting up by adding the same number over and over. Skip counting by 2's means 2, 4, 6, etc. Practice skip counting 2's and 3's and you will be able to multiply faster than a horde of zombie bunnies!

2's: 2, 4, 6, 8, 10, 12, 14, 16, 18, 20, 22, 24.

3's: 3, 6, 9, 12, 15, 18, 21, 24, 27, 30, 33, 36.

Great Work Today! See you tomorrow, Math Master!

Day 2

Use Your Tools!

Use your multiplication skills to answer this question. (Remember you can use repeated addition to answer any multiplication problem!)

The school roller skating night is in 3 weeks. You want to bring at least $10 so that you have enough money to buy tons of candy AND play air hockey until Jessie W. begs for mercy. You can earn $4 per week if you take out the trash AND do the dishes every night (UGH!). How much money will you have at the skating rink if you earn $4 each week for 3 weeks?

Build Your Skills!

Remember skip counting? Prove it! Skip count by 2's right here.

2's: 2, 4 , 6 , 8 , 10 , 12 , 14 , 16 , 18 , 20 , 22 , 24 .

Now use skip counting to fill in this multiplication matrix.

	X 1	X 2	X 3	X 4	X 5	X 6	X 7	X 8	X 9	X 10	X 11	X 12
2:	2	4	6	8	10	12	14	16	18	20	22	24

Work It Out!

2 X 4 = 8	3 X 7 = 21	2 X 10 = 20
2 X 12 = 24	3 X 5 = 15	2 X 2 = 4
3 X 6 = 18	1 X 10 = 10	3 X 8 = 24
3 X 7 = 21	2 X 8 = 16	9 X 3 = 24

Fast Facts!

Write your 2's multiplication facts, fast as you can! Have someone time you!

2 X 1 = 2	2 X 5 = 10	2 X 9 = 18
2 X 2 = 4	2x 6=12	2x10=20
2x3=6	2x 7=14	2x11=22
2x 4=8	2x 8=16	2x12=24

Time: 52 seconds

Great work today, Math Wiz! Keep it Up!

Day 3

Warm-Up!

Fill in the 2's chart from yesterday, but this time add 3's!

	X 1	X 2	X 3	X 4	X 5	X 6	X 7	X 8	X 9	X 10	X 11	X 12
2:	2	4	6	8	10	12	14	16	18	20	22	24
3:	3	6	9	12	15	18	21	24	27	30	33	36

Lets Learn Something!

Here's another multiplication hack for you. It's called Circle and Dot. When you need to multiply 2 X 6, you draw 2 circles and put 6 dots in each. Then you just count the dots to find the answer!

Work It Out!

Daredevil Park is the best park in town! It has 4 Merry-Go-Rounds! If 5 kids can fit on each Merry-Go-Round, how many kids can play on Merry-Go-Rounds at one time? Use the circle/dot method!

Fast Facts!

Write your 2's multiplication facts, fast as you can! See if you can beat yesterday's time?

2 X 1 = 2	2 X 5 = 10	2 X 9 = 18
2 X 2 = 4	2x6=12	2x10=20
2x3=6	2x7=14	2x11=22
2x4=8	2x8=16	2x12=24

Time: 41 seconds

Build Your Skill!

Use your either the circle/dot method or repeated addition to crush these multiplication problems!

3 X 9 = 9+9+9=24	2 X 11 = 11+11=22
3 X 12 = 12+12+12=36	2 X 9 = 9+9=18

Cool Fact: One way to practice skip counting threes is to sing them to the tune of Jingle Bells. (Use the "Batman smells" version, if you must.)

Try it. It is fun!

3-6-9, 12-15, 18-21, 24 and 27, 30 and you're done - HEY!

Awesome job! See you tomorrow, Mathinator!

Day 4

Day 4 is all about-- well you guessed it -- 4! Use skip counting to complete the 2's and 4's multiplication matrices.

	X 1	X 2	X 3	X 4	X 5	X 6	X 7	X 8	X 9	X 10	X 11	X 12
2:	2	4	6	8	10	12	14	16	18	20	22	24
4:	4	8	12	16	20	24	28	32	36	40	44	48

Cool Fact: An easy way to think of your four facts is to double the answer from the same 2's fact.

So for 4 X 6, first think of 2 X 6 = 12. Then double 12 and you get 24.

So, 4 X 6 = 24.

Check it out in the chart above!

Fast Facts!

Its **time** for a **times** test! See if you can answer these 20 questions in under a minute! We're going for speed over accuracy here so even if you aren't 100% sure, just go with your instinct!

2 X 6 = 12	2 X 8 = 16	2 X 9 = 18
2 X 2 = 4	2 X 4 = 8	2 X 5 = 10
2 X 5 = 16	2 X 12 = 24	2 X 7 = 14
2 X 3 = 6	2 X 1 = 2	2 X 8 = 16
2 X 7 = 14	2 X 3 = 6	2 X 4 = 8
2 X 9 = 18	2 X 6 = 12	2 X 12 = 24
2 X 10 = 20	2 X 11 = 22	FINISHED!

Time: ____________

Use Your Tools!

On the planet, Mathos, all the way on the other side of the Universe, the Emperor Zorbo is building an army of squirrels to invade earth. (Sounds nuts, but hey- it wasn't *my* plan.) Zorbo uses a cloning machine that multiplies whoever he sends in. If the dial is set to 2X then 2 squirrels become 4 and 8 squirrels become 16. Calculate how many squirrels Zorbo will have using the In/Out machines below.

IN		OUT
2		4
3	Dial Shows 2X.....	6
4		8
5		16
6		12

IN		OUT
3		9
4	Dial Shows 3X.....	12
5		15
6		18
7		21

IN		OUT
2		8
3	Dial Shows 4X.....	12
4		16
5		26
6		24

IN		OUT
8		24
9	Dial Shows 3X.....	24
10		30
11		33
12		36

Good math-ing today, young one! Good Math-ing!

Day 5
Build Your Skills!

Welcome to the Matrix! Use these charts to practice build your fluency.

X	1	2	3
1	1	2	3
2	2	4	6
3	3	6	9

The outside numbers are factors.

X	1	2	3
1	1	2	3
2	2	4	6
3	3	6	9

Follow the row of one factor.

X	1	2	3
1	1	2	3
2	2	4	6
3	3	6	9

Multiplied by the column of the other factor.

Fill in these tables for a great multiplication work out!

X	2	3	4
2	4	6	8
3	6	9	12
4	8	12	16

X	8	9	10
2	16	18	20
3	24	27	30
4	32	36	40

X	5	6	7
2	10	12	14
3	15	18	21
4	20	24	28

Let's Learn Something!

That Zorbo is at it again! When the squirrel army didn't work out he invented the Zero-inator! It turns out that whenever you multiply something by zero, the answer is ALWAYS ZERO!

6 lovely trees X 0 = 0 lovely trees

12 puny humans X 0 = 0 puny humans

10,000 army tanks X 0 = 0 army tanks

Anything X 0 = 0 anything!

Cool, right?!

I mean, when it's not in the hands of an evil ruler.

Fast Facts!

Write your 3's multiplication facts, fast as you can! 1-12. Don't forget to time yourself so you can track your progress!

3 X 1 = 3	3x5=15	3x9=27
3 X 2 = 6	3x6=18	3x10=30
3x3=9	3x7=21	3x11=33
3x4=12	3x8=24	3x12=36

Time: 1 minute

Great work today! Catch you later!

Day 6

Cool Fact: Have you noticed the answer to both 2 X 3 and 3 X 2 is 6? That is because multiplication is commutative (come-mute-a-tiv), meaning that it doesn't matter what order the numbers are in, the answer will always be the same. Addition is also commutative (8 + 2 = 10 and 2 + 8 = 10), while subtraction is not (8 - 2 = 6 and 2 - 8 = is impossible with positive numbers.)

Work It Out!

Use repeated addition to see the commutative property at work in these problems! Draw lines to connect the boxes with the same answers.

2 X 4 =	3 X 7 =	12 X 3 =
7 X 3 =	3 X 5 =	3 X 9 =
3 X 6 =	3 X 12 =	4 X 2 =
5 X 3 =	6 X 3 =	9 X 3 =

Fast Facts!

Write your 3's multiplication facts, fast as you can! 1-12. Don't forget to time yourself so you can track your progress!

3 X 1 = 3	3x5=15	3x9=27
3 X 2 =6	3x6=18	3x10=36
3x3=9	3x7=21	3x11=33
3x4=12	3x8=24	3x12=36

Time: 1 min 10 sec

Use Your Tools!

Morris has a best friend Molly who only likes the peanut butter insides of her peanut butter cracker sandwiches. Luckily, Morris, only likes the cracker outsides! (This is why they are best friends, duh!)

Today, Molly brought a 6 pack of peanut butter cracker sandwiches to school. How many crackers will Morris get from Molly? You can use line/dot, repeated addition, or your 2's facts to answer this question.

6 ÷ 2=3 Morris will get 3 crackers

You are on a roll, Math Star! See you tomorrow!

Day 7

Warm It Up!

Use skip counting to fill in the matrix.

	X 1	X 2	X 3	X 4	X 5	X 6	X 7	X 8	X 9	X 10	X 11	X 12
2:	2	4	6	8	10	12	14	16	18	20	22	24
3:	3	6	9	12	15	18	21	24	27	30	33	36
4:	4	8	12	16	20	24	28	32	36	40	44	48
5:	5	10	15	20	25	30	35	40	45	50	55	60

Lets Learn Something!

A number line is a great way to ***see*** multiplication. Of course, we're going to do it the "Rowdy Kids" way. Here we go!

Owen, child genius, is working on a water-balloon cannon that uses super-strong water-balloons that bounce a set number times (and spaces) before they explode. In the first test, the balloon bounced 5 spaces 4 times. Use the number line to find out how many total spaces the balloon traveled.

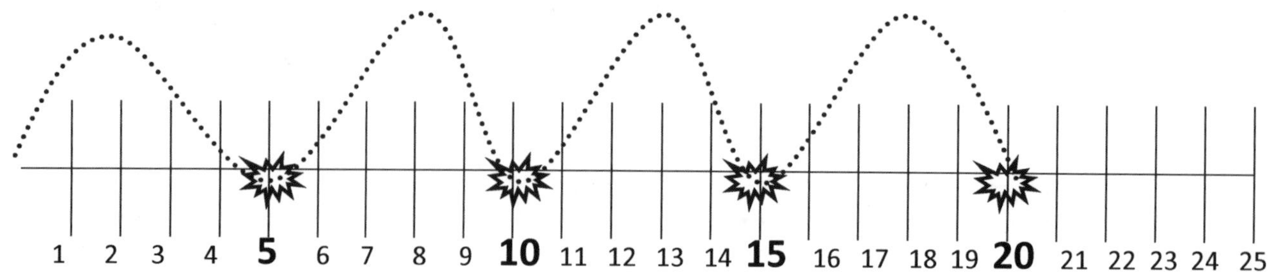

Work It Out!

Use the number line to solve these word problems.

1. Owen has adjusted his water balloon cannon so that it now bounces 3 spaces each time. If balloon bounces 4 times, how many spaces will it go?

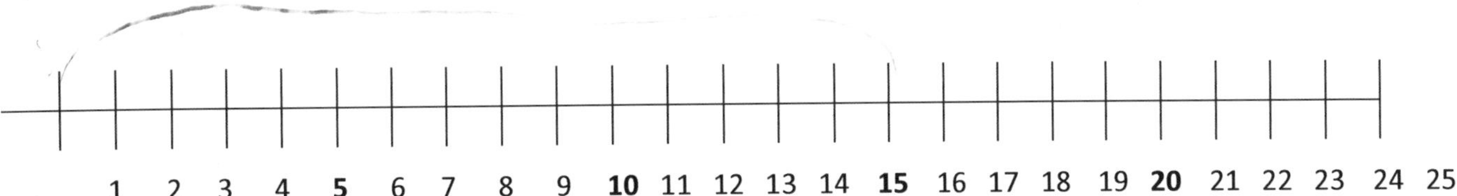

2. Unfortunately, Owen's little brother, Orion, got a hold of the cannon. Now any balloon that is shot out of there goes 11 spaces with each bounce but it can only bounce 2 times. How far will the water balloon travel?

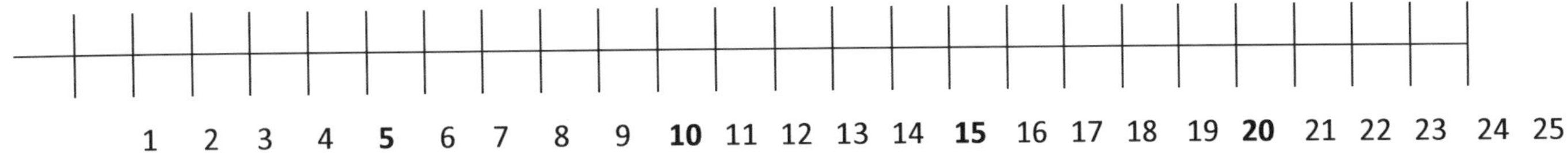

Fast Facts!

Time: 50 sec

See if you can answer these 20 questions in under a minute!

3 X 5 = 15	3 X 12 = 36	3 X 7 = 21	3 X 10 = 36	9 X 3 = 24
3 X 3 = 9	3 X 1 = 3	8 X 3 = 24	5 X 3 = 15	1 X 3 = 3
7 X 3 = 21	2 X 3 = 6	3 X 4 = 12	11 X 3 = 33	6 X 3 = 18
3 X 9 = 27	3 X 6 = 18	12 X 3 = 36	3 X 2 = 6	3 X 8 = 24

Wonderful work, Math Warrior! See you tomorrow!

Day 8

Lets Learn Something!

Zorbo's cloning machine has gotten out of control and he doesn't know how many squirrels are in his squirrel army. Lucky for him, he can use ARRAYS to find out.

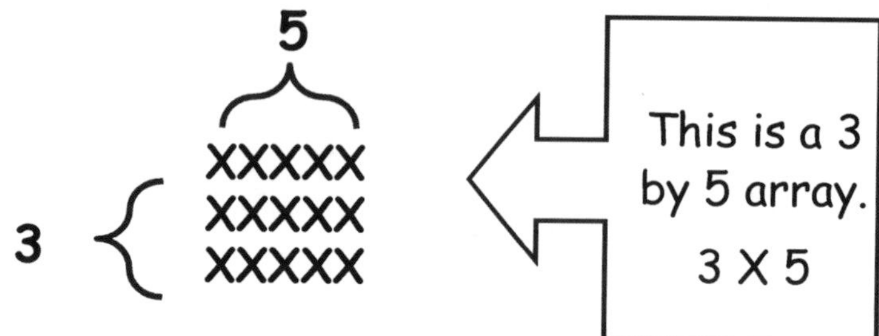

Just count the x's to find the answer! 3 X 5 = 15.

Work It Out!

Use arrays to find the answers to the problems below. Just think about all of those squirrel uniforms Zorbo is going to have to order!

5 X 4 =	3 X 7 =	10 X 4 =
4 X 3 =	4 X 9 =	5 X 11 =
3 X 6 =	4 X 4 =	4 X 12 =

Build Your Skills!

Fill in the matrices as fast as you can!

X	0	1	2
2			
3			
4			

X	3	4	5
3			
4			
5			

X	5	6	7
3			
4			
5			

Flex 'Em!

Penny and her sister Peaches were having a bouncy-ball bouncing contest in the living room while their parents were finishing breakfast. On Penny's turn the ball bounced 3 times, travelling 6 feet each time, landing directly in her mother's coffee cup after the last bounce.

Use the number line to determine exactly how many feet Penny's ball bounced before landing her in a BIG mess!

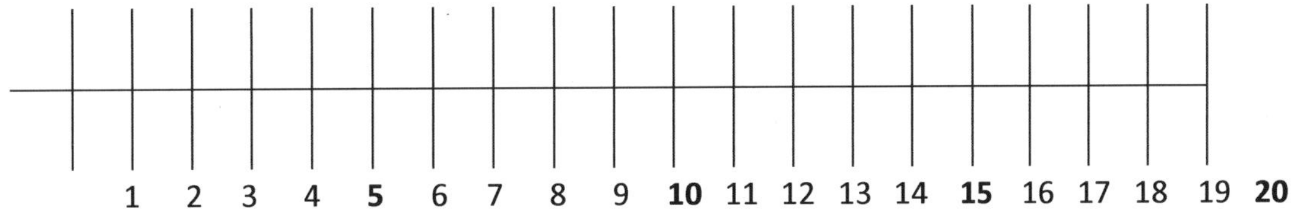

Wonderful work, Math Warrior! See you tomorrow!

Day 9

Build Your Skills!

Lets mix it up a bit. Fill in the open boxes of this multiplication matrix. *(HINT: It's OK to say the numbers that go in the blacked-out spaces in your head. No one will ever know... Except your mom, who seems to know everything.)*

	X 1	X 2	X 3	X 4	X 5	X 6	X 7	X 8	X 9	X 10	X 11	X 12
2:												
3:												
4:												
5:												

Cool Fact: To **multiply by 10** you just take the other factor and add a zero. So...

6 X 10 = 60

3 X 10 = 30

ETC. ETC.

You just learned a whole fact family, just like that! **Sweet!**

Jack is selling candy bars to earn money to go on the pig racing field trip. (Don't ask). He needs $45 if he wants to name his own pig. (Seriously, don't ask). Each box has 8 candy bars in it that each sell for $1. He has already sold 4 boxes. Does he have enough money? (Use arrays, circle/dot, repeated addition or the double 2's trick to solve this problem.)

Fast Facts!

Write your 4's multiplication facts, fast as you can! 1-12. Don't forget to time yourself so you can track your progress!

4 X 1 = 4		
4 X 2 =		

Time: ___________

Work It Out!

Use arrays or circle/dot to find the answers to the problems below.

5 X 6 =	3 X 4 =	12 X 4 =
7 X 5 =	2 X 5 =	3 X 9 =
5 X 8 =	3 X 11 =	5 X 7 =

You are crushing it! Great work today, Math Kid!

Day 10

Fast Facts!

Take another shot at these 3's facts! Remember, speed first!
See if you can answer these 20 questions in under a minute!

3 X 5 =	3 X 12 =	3 X 7 =	3 X 10 =	9 X 3 =
3 X 3 =	3 X 1 =	8 X 3 =	5 X 3 =	1 X 3 =
7 X 3 =	2 X 3 =	3 X 4 =	11 X 3 =	6 X 3 =
3 X 9 =	3 X 6 =	12 X 3 =	3 X 2 =	3 X 8 =

Time: __________

Work It Out!

Jenny is selling friendship bracelets for $1 each. She is wondering how much more money she'll make if she raises the price to $3 or $4. Complete the in and out boxes below to determine how much she will make if she sells bracelets at different prices.

IN		OUT
2	$3 per bracelet	
3		
4		
5		
6		

IN		OUT
2	$4 per bracelet	
3		
4		
5		
6		

Use Your Tools!

Billy and Booster are programming robots to bring them popcorn while they play in a Slap Jack tournament. (A card game where the person who slaps the jack gets all the cards.) Each robot can only travel 4 feet. How far will 4 robots get them? How many different ways can you think to solve this problem?

Booster spends the morning upgrading the robots so that they can travel 6 feet in one run. Now, how far can 4 robots get them?

The robots can bring 5 cups of popcorn per trip. If they make 7 trips, how much popcorn do Billy and Booster get to eat?

Good Workout! Stay with it, Math Monster!

Day 11

Warm It Up!

Today we'll add 6's to the mix!

	X 1	X 2	X 3	X 4	X 5	X 6	X 7	X 8	X 9	X 10	X 11	X 12
3:												
4:												
5:												
6:												

Cool Fact: When multiplying 5's the product always ends in either 5 or 0.

Also, you can take the factor times 10 and cut it in half.

So...

5 X 8 = ?

10 X 8 = 80

Half of 80 is 40.

5 X 8 = 40

Use Your Tools!

Lily is planning a surprise for her mother's birthday party. She and her sisters are going to shoot off fireworks as her mom comes into the backyard. If there are 5 sisters in total and they each shoot off 6 firecrackers, how many firecrackers will there be? Use arrays to answer this question.

Build Your Skills!

Fill in these matrices to strengthen your math muscles!

X	0	1	2
3			
4			
5			

X	3	4	5
4			
5			
6			

X	6	7	8
4			
5			
6			

X	0	1	2
0			
1			
2			

X	9	10	11
3			
4			
5			

X	10	11	12
4			
5			
6			

Fast Facts!

See how fast you can write your 4's facts! Time yourself so that you can track your progress! Time:_______

4 X 1 = 4		
4 X 2=		

That's all for today! Great work, Math-inator!

Day 12

Fast Facts!

Time for a 4's facts times test! Go with your gut and see if you can answer these 20 questions in under a minute!

4 X 5 =	4 X 12 =	3 X 4 =	4 X 10 =	9 X 4 =
4 X 3 =	4 X 7 =	8 X 4 =	5 X 4 =	1 X 4 =
7 X 4 =	2 X 4 =	3 X 4 =	11 X 4 =	6 X 4 =
4 X 4 =	4 X 6 =	12 X 4 =	4 X 2 =	4 X 8 =

Time: __________

Build Your Skills!

Use skip counting to fill in the open boxes of this multiplication matrix. Don't fall into the holes!

	X 1	X 2	X 3	X 4	X 5	X 6	X 7	X 8	X 9	X 10	X 11	X 12
3:												
4:												
5:												
6:												

Work It Out!

Olly won the lottery and with his winnings he bought an entire truck full of foot-long bubble gum roll-ups! Each package contains 6 feet of bubble gum! (That's as tall as a full grown horse!) Being a nice guy, Olly gave boxes of gum to all of his friends. Use arrays to find out how many feet of bubble gum he gave to each of his friends.

5 X 6 = feet of gum for Miles	**6 X 4 =** feet of gum for Betsy	**12 X 6 =** feet of gum for Asher
6 X 5 = feet of gum for Malik	**2 X 6 =** feet of gum for Jaden	**6 X 9 =** feet of gum for Belle
6 X 8 = feet of gum for Emma	**6 X 11 =** feet of gum for Drew	**6 X 7 =** feet of gum for Henry

Cool Fact: In multiplication you can use the **distributive property** to help simplify some problems. 2 X 12 is the same as 2 X (2 + 10) which is the same as (2 x 10) + (2 x 2). The 2 is ***distributed*** to each of the factors. Work it out and see for yourself!

Great progress, Math Maniac!

Day 13

Use Your Tools!

Samantha is having a scavenger hunt birthday party and she has invited 8 friends! The first stop is the ice cream shop. If all 9 friends get a triple scoop ice cream cone, how many total scoops of ice cream will the scoopers scoop? Use circle/dot to answer this question.

The next stop on the birthday tour is the park where the girls are playing a game of giant marbles. At the beginning of the game each of the 9 girls starts with 5 "marbles." (These are really just huge beach balls.) How many marbles are there?

As a party gift Samantha gave each of her 8 friends 6 tadpoles! If all goes well in a few weeks there will be how many frogs hopping all around?

Fast Facts!

Let's take another shot at those 4's facts!

See if you can answer these 20 questions in under a minute!

4 X 7 =	4 X 2 =	5 X 4 =	4 X 12 =	11 X 4 =
4 X 5 =	4 X 9 =	10 X 4 =	7 X 4 =	3 X 4 =
9 X 4 =	4 X 4 =	4 X 4 =	1 X 4 =	8 X 4 =
6 X 4 =	4 X 8 =	12 X 4 =	4 X 4 =	4 X 10 =

Time: __________

Build Your Skills!

Fill in the open boxes on this multiplication matrix. Don't step on the crack or you'll... (I can't remember how it goes from there, you finish it!)

	X 1	X 2	X 3	X 4	X 5	X 6	X 7	X 8	X 9	X 10	X 11	X 12
2:												
3:												
4:												
5:												
6:												

Keep at it, Math Star!

Day 14
Fast Facts!

Write your 5's multiplication facts, fast as you can! 1-12. Don't forget to time yourself so you can track your progress!

5 X 1 = 5		
5 X 2 =		

Time: __________

Work It Out!

Alton is trying to predict how much money he will make from selling his super-awesome lemonade made from his super-awesome, super-secret recipe at the 3rd Grade fundraiser. Of course it all depends on how much he charges per cup AND how many cups he sells. Use the In/Out machine to calculate his possible contributions.

IN		OUT
2	$5 per cup	
3		
4		
5		
6		

IN		OUT
2	$6 per cup	
3		
4		
5		
6		

Flex 'Em!

Ricky is entering his pet rabbit, Fluffers, in the county bunny race. The race course is 20 feet long. At the start of training Fluffers traveled 2 feet with every jump. How many jumps did it take Fluffers to reach the end of the course? Use the number line to answer this question.

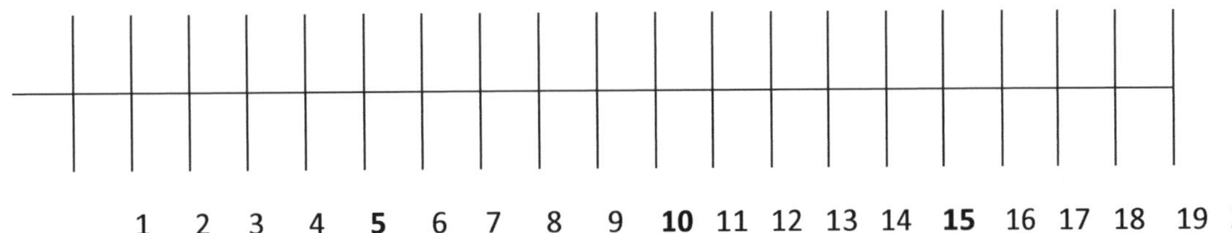

Ricky's creative training program has doubled Fluffers the length of each of Fluffers' jumps 4 feet. (It's amazing what a nice big juicy carrot on top of the washing machine will do for a bunnie's effort level!) Now how many jumps does it take for Fluffers to reach the finish line?

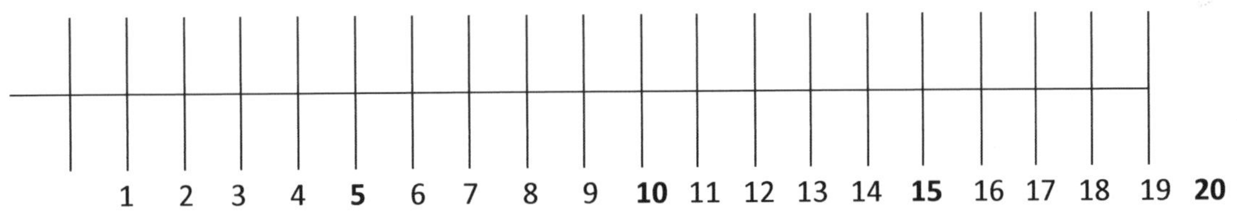

Fun Alert! Dominos War! To play, flip your dominos upside down and divide them evenly between all players. During each round, the players flip a domino into the middle of the table, multiply the two sides of their domino. Whoever has the highest product gets to keep the dominos. Continue until one player has all of the dominos. Its War!

Good workout! Flex those math muscles!

Day 15
Work It Out!

Lily loves chocolate chip cookies. But she is very particular about how they are made. Lily likes to have exactly 6 chocolate chips on each of her cookies. Use circle/dot to find out how many chocolate chips Lily will need if she makes different amounts of cookies.

6 X 6 =	6 X 11 =	6 X 8 =
6 X 3 =	6 X 2 =	6 X 12 =
6 X 9 =	6 X 4 =	6 X 7 =

Cool Fact: You can use the commutative property to make multiplication problems easier. Since 2 X 12 is the same thing as 12 X 2 you can draw 2 circles and put 12 dots inside to answer either question. Or just add 12 + 12 instead of adding 2 a gazillion (if by gazillion you mean 12) times!

Fast Facts!

Let's take another shot at those 4's facts!

See if you can answer these 20 questions in under a minute!

4 X 6 =	4 X 1 =	4 X 4 =	4 X 11 =	10 X 4 =
4 X 4 =	4 X 8 =	9 X 4 =	6 X 4 =	2 X 4 =
8 X 4 =	3 X 4 =	4 X 5 =	12 X 4 =	7 X 4 =
5 X 4 =	4 X 7 =	1 X 4 =	4 X 3 =	4 X 9 =

Time: __________

Use Your Tools!

Peter Piper picked a peck of pickled peppers. Actually, let's say that Peter Piper picked 6 pecks of pickled peppers. If each peck has 12 peppers how many pickled peppers did Peter Piper pick? (Say that 6 times fast, I dare you!) Use arrays or circle/dot to answer this question.

Nice! Your math skills are getting super pumped!

Day 16
Build Your Skills!

Fill in these math matrices to work on your fluency. Let's Go!

X	4	5	6
4			
5			
6			

X	4	5	6
10			
11			
12			

X	4	5	6
7			
8			
9			

Fast Facts!

Write your 5's multiplication facts, fast as you can! 1-12. Time yourself so you can track your progress!

5 X 1 = 5		
5 X 2 =		

Time: ___________

Use Your Tools!

Maya and Mario have discovered that they can use their roller skates to transport tiny cups of water from the bathroom to the action figure party that they are having in their playroom. Maya and Marion each have one pair of skates. If they can balance 5 cups on each skate, how may cups can they bring in one trip? Use arrays to answer this question.

Maya and Mario's mother found out about their plan to use the skates. Needless to say, she did not think it was such a great idea. Now they are bringing the cups to their playroom by balancing them on their hands. If they can balance only 3 cups on each hand, how many cups can they bring in one trip. Use arrays to answer this question.

You're crushing it, Math Magician!

Day 17

Fast Facts!

Write your 6's multiplication facts, fast as you can! 1-12. Time yourself so that you can track your progress!

6 X 1 = 6		
6 X 2 =		

Time: __________

Work It Out!

Esther's parents have made her a deal. For every dirty sock that she picks up from the floor she gets 5 jelly beans and for every handful of legos she gets 6 jelly beans. Luckily for Esther, her room is a huge mess! Use the in and out boxes to see how many jelly beans she will get for cleaning her room.

IN	socks	OUT
8	5 jelly beans	
9		
10		
11		
12		

IN	Legos	OUT
8	6 jelly beans	
9		
10		
11		
12		

Build Your Skills!

Use skip-counting to fill in the matrix below.

	X 2	X 3	X 4	X 5	X 6	X 7	X 8	X 9	X 10	X 11	X 12
0:											
1:											
2:											
3:											
4:											
5:											
6:											
7:											

Cool Fact: To find 6's facts use what you know about 5 and add one more group.

To find 6 X 4:

First find 5 X 4 = 20.

Then add one more 4.

20 + 4 = 24.

6 X 4 = 24.

Can you do it with another one? 6 X 7= ?

Way to work, Math-osaurus Rex!

Day 18

Multiplication Maze!

Make it through this maze using your multiplication facts. Don't get lost!

		1	2	3	4	5	6	7	8	9	10	
	0											
	1											
Start!	2											
	3											
	4											End!
	5											
	6											

Fast Facts!

Its time for a 5's time test!

See if you can answer these 20 questions in under a minute!

5 X 6 =	5 X 1 =	5 X 5 =	5 X 11 =	10 X 5 =
5 X 4 =	5 X 8 =	9 X 5 =	6 X 5 =	2 X 5 =
8 X 5 =	3 X 5 =	6 X 5 =	12 X 5 =	7 X 5 =
5 X 5 =	5 X 7 =	1 X 5 =	5 X 3 =	5 X 9 =

Time: __________

Let's Learn Something!

Let's say you want to cover the floor in your room entirely with marshmallows. (Hey, it wasn't my idea!) How do you know how many marshmallows to get from the store? The key to this question is **area.** Area is measured in **square feet-** which literally means a square where each side is a foot.

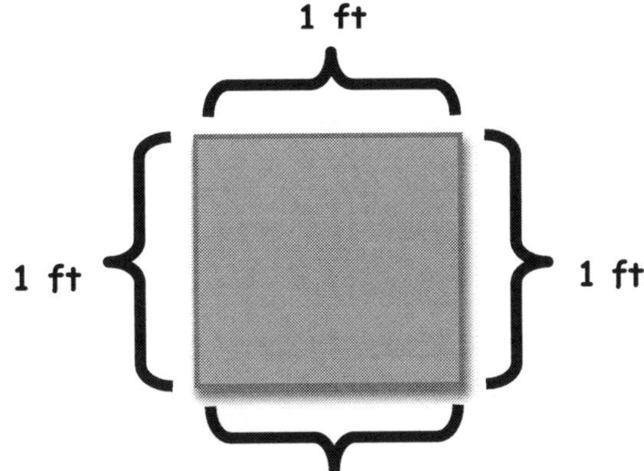

1 ft

You find the area of any rectangle by multiplying:

Width X Height

In the case of our square it would be: 1ft X 1ft = 1 square foot.

What is the area of this rectangle?

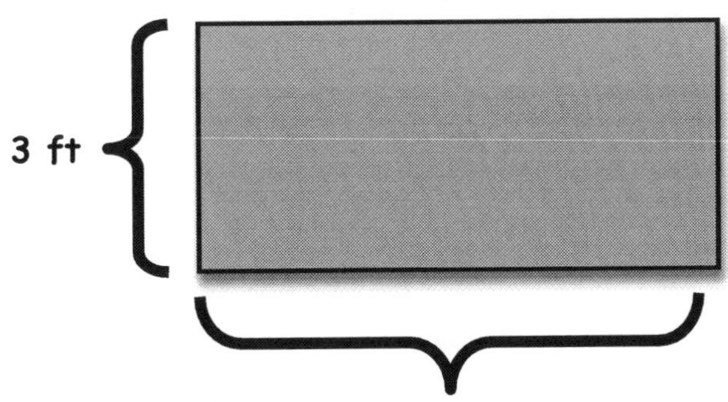

6 ft

HINT: The Width is 6ft and the Height is 3 ft.

Amazing Work Today!

Day 19

Fast Facts!

Write your 6's multiplication facts, fast as you can! 1-12. Don't forget to time yourself so you can track your progress!

6 X 1 = 6		
6 X 2 =		

Time: ___________

Work It Out!

Morris and Stacey are arguing over the perfect size for a guinea pig cage. Morris thinks they need at least 40 square feet while Stacey thinks they can get away with 20 square feet. Use arrays to determine how many square feet each of the following possible cage dimensions.

6ft X 7ft	**7ft X 11ft**	**7ft X 8ft**
7ft X 3ft	**7ft X 2ft**	**7ft X 12ft**

Build Your Skills!

Fill in these math matrices to work on your fluency. Come on, you can do it!

X	5	6	7
4			
5			
6			

X	5	6	7
10			
11			
12			

X	5	6	7
7			
8			
9			

Flex 'Em!

Jonas's mother claims that every square foot of his bed is completely covered in stuffed animals. According to his calculations, Jonas's bed is 3 ft wide by 7 ft long. How many square feet is covered by stuffed animals? Go ahead and draw the rectangle if you want to *see* the math in action!

You are the mathiest, Mathy McMathikins!!

Day 20

Work It Out!

Flip the script and find the missing factors in these multiplication Matrix! Then complete the matrix.

X	0		
7	0		
		8	
			18

X			
	36		
		50	
			66

X			
			120
		121	
	120		

X			
			0
		3	
	4		

X			
			10
		12	
	12		

X			
	36		
		49	
			64

Cool Fact: Trying to multiply 8's? Try the double-double trick! 8 is 2 doubled and then doubled again... 2 + 2 = 4 and 4 + 4 = 8. Then we can find any product of 8 by first doubling the other factor and then doubling it again!

What about 8 X 6? First: 2 X 6 = 12

Double it: 12 +12 = 24 Double it Again!: 24 + 24 = 48

8 X 6 = 48!

Fast Facts!

Its time for a 6's time test!

See if you can answer these 20 questions in under a minute!

6 X 6 =	6 X 1 =	6 X 5 =	6 X 11 =	10 X 6 =
6 X 4 =	6 X 8 =	9 X 6 =	6 X 8 =	2 X 6 =
8 X 6 =	3 X 6 =	6 X 6 =	12 X 6 =	7 X 6 =
5 X 6 =	6 X 7 =	1 X 6 =	6 X 3 =	6 X 9 =

Time: ________

Use Your Tools!

Micah and his family are at the beach and he and his brother, Mo, are building the world's largest sand castle! (At least, they can't imagine a sand castle bigger than this, that is.) The moat around the castle is a rectangle that is 6 feet wide and 12 feet long. How many square feet are included in the Royal Sand Empire? Use arrays to answer this question.

You knocked it out (as usual), Math Master!

Day 21
Fast Facts!

Write your 7's multiplication facts, fast as you can! 1-12. Don't forget to time yourself so you can track your progress!

7 X 1 = 7		
7 X 2 =		

Time: __________

Work It Out!

Leo worked out a deal with his big sister: for every pony-tail holder he found she would give him 7 minutes of her weekday gaming time or 8 minutes of her weekend gaming time. Use the In/Out machine to determine how many minutes he might earn with different numbers of pony-tail holders.

IN		OUT
3	7 minutes	
4		
5		
6		
7		

IN		OUT
3	8 minutes	
4		
5		
6		
7		

Multiplication Maze!

Make it through this maze using your multiplication facts. Don't get lost!

		1	2	3	4	5	6	7	8	9	10	
	1											
	2											
Start!	3											
	4											End!
	5											
	6											
	7											

Use Your Tools!

Kristi's dog Bruno collects socks and hides them under one of his 3 dog beds. If there are 12 socks under each bed, how many individual socks does Bruno have? Try using the distributive property to answer this question. HINT: How could you break up 12 to make the multiplication easier?

Great work today, Math Wiz! Keep it Up!

Day 22

Build Your Skills!

Fill in the open boxes on this multiplication matrix. Don't step on the crack or you'll... start singing show-tunes and hopping on one leg? (Nope, not it)

	X 1	X 2	X 3	X 4	X 5	X 6	X 7	X 8	X 9	X 10	X 11	X 12
3:												
4:												
5:												
6:												
7:												

Fast Facts!

Its time for a 6's time test! Faster the better.

See if you can answer these 20 questions in under a minute!

6 X 6 =	6 X 1 =	6 X 5 =	6 X 11 =	10 X 6 =
6 X 4 =	6 X 8 =	9 X 6 =	6 X 8 =	2 X 6 =
8 X 6 =	3 X 6 =	6 X 6 =	12 X 6 =	7 X 6 =
5 X 6 =	6 X 7 =	1 X 6 =	6 X 3 =	6 X 9 =

Time: ___________

Use Your Tools!

Anthony and Stella are preparing for the summer block-party by creating a **human** bowling lane in their front yard! Regulation human bowling lanes must be 3ft X 10ft long. What area must they cover with soap to make the entire lane super slippery? Use arrays to answer this question.

To kick things up they turn their regular sized lane into a jumbo lane! A jumbo human bowling lane is 6ft wide and 24ft long! How much area does the land cover now? Use the distributive function to answer this question.

Great progress, Math Maniac!

Day 23

Let's Learn Something!

The distributive function is pretty handy for breaking a big multiplication problem into bite size pieces . Let's look at the last question from yesterday's workout. To find the area of the jumbo human bowling lane we needed to multiply 6 X 24.

STEP 1: Break down the large factor into easy to multiply parts.

24 = 10 + 10 + 4

(I used 10's because they are super easy to multiply!)

STEP 2: Rewrite the problem to show the broken-down factors.

6 X (10 + 10 + 4)

STEP 3: Distribute the remaining factor among the new "pieces."

(6 X 10) + (6 X 10) + (6 X 4)

Now you've got three easier problems instead of one harder one!

STEP 4: Solve the problems!

6 X 10 = 60

6 X 10 = 60

6 X 4 = +24

144

Now that you know that trick, every multiplication problem is solvable!

Fast Facts!

Write your 7's multiplication facts, fast as you can! 1-12. Don't forget to time yourself so you can track your progress!

7 X 1 = 7		
7 X 2 =		

Time: ___________

Work It Out!

Flip the script and find the missing factors in these multiplication Matrix! Then complete the matrix.

X			
	24		
		35	
			48

X			
	45		
		60	
			77

X			
	12		
		21	
			32

Wonderful work, today!

Day 24

Build Your Skills!

Use skip counting to fill in the multiplication matrix below. Did you notice we added 8's? We're up to 8's, Math-Star!

	X 1	X 2	X 3	X 4	X 5	X 6	X 7	X 8	X 9	X 10	X 11	X 12
6:												
7:												
8:												

Let's Learn Something!

Did you know the distributive function can be used with arrays?! Check it!

This is a 4 X 15 matrix.

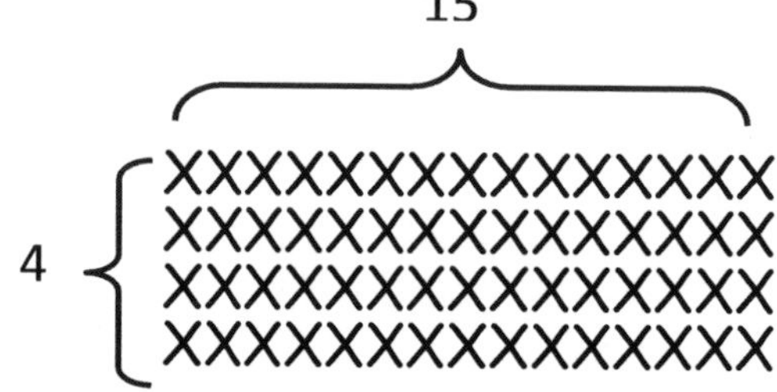

Now let's break down the 15 into smaller pieces: 5 + 10!

	5			10	
4	XXXXX XXXXX XXXXX XXXXX	+	4	XXXXXXXXXX XXXXXXXXXX XXXXXXXXXX XXXXXXXXXX	=
	20	**+**		**40**	**= 60**

Work It Out!

Make distributive arrays to answer the following questions.
If it helps, you can imagine that each X marks a buried treasure!
Not sure why that would help, but, whatever.

8 X 6 =	8 X 11 =
8 X 9 =	8 X 12 =

Fast Facts!

Its time for a 7's time test! Remember: speed is the goal!
See if you can answer these 20 questions in under a minute!

7 X 6 =	7 X 1 =	7 X 5 =	7 X 11 =	10 X 7 =
7 X 4 =	7 X 8 =	9 X 7 =	7 X 8 =	2 X 7 =
8 X 7 =	3 X 7 =	6 X 7 =	12 X 7 =	7 X 7 =
5 X 7 =	7 X 7 =	1 X 7 =	7 X 3 =	7 X 9 =

Time: ___________

You are kicking major math, kid!

Day 25

Build Your Skills!

Use skip counting to fill in the open boxes of this multiplication matrix. Don't fall into the holes!

	1	2	3	4	5	6	7	8	9	10	11	12
5:												
6:												
7:												
8:												

Work It Out!

Alaster is working on his basketball skills. To keep it interesting he draws two cards and multiplies them together to determine how many times he has to dribble the ball up and down the sidewalk in front of his house. Jacks = 11, Queen = 12, King = 13. Work out how many trips Alaster has to make for each draw below. Use arrays to answer the questions below.

4 X 8 =	6 X 11 =	7 X 9 =

Fast Facts!

Write your 8's multiplication facts, fast as you can! 1-12. Don't forget to time yourself so you can track your progress!

8 X 1 = 8		
8 X 2 =		

Time: ___________

Work It Out!

Zorbo is back with his cloning machine! This time he is cloning carrot cupcakes in an attempt to lure unsuspecting health-nuts into a trap. How many cupcakes will he make if he sets the dial to 7 and 8.

IN		OUT
8	Dial at 7	
9		
10		
11		
12		

IN		OUT
8	Dial at 8	
9		
10		
11		
12		

Something's happening here, Math Manager!

Day 26

Fast Facts!

Its time for a 7's time test!

See if you can answer these 20 questions in under a minute!

7 X 6 =	7 X 1 =	7 X 5 =	7 X 11 =	10 X 7 =
7 X 4 =	7 X 8 =	9 X 7 =	7 X 8 =	2 X 7 =
8 X 7 =	3 X 7 =	6 X 7 =	12 X 7 =	7 X 7 =
5 X 7 =	7 X 7 =	1 X 7 =	7 X 3 =	7 X 9 =

Time: __________

Multiplication Maze!

		1	2	3	4	5	6	7	8	9	10	
	1											End!
	2											
	3											
	4											
	5											
Start!	6											
	7											

Use Your Tools!

Makayla and Trey are planning to sign up for the school talent show but they know that to win they have to do something BIG! So the current plan is to learn to juggle donuts. For the routine both Makayla and Trey need 8 boxes of 12 donuts. How many total donuts do they need? Use the distributive property to answer this question.

After the show, Makayla ate 2 boxes and Trey ate 4. How many total donuts did they eat together?

Their friends, Tina and Theresa, had best performance. They trained frogs to turn bicycle pedals! (You had to see it to believe it! It took 7 frogs to ride one bike. If there were 12 bikes how many frogs would that take?

Great job today, Math Wiz!

Day 27

Fast Facts!

Write your 8's multiplication facts, fast as you can! 1-12. Don't forget to time yourself so you can track your progress!

8 X 1 = 8		
8 X 2 =		

Time: __________

Flex 'Em!

A giraffe is going jogging (bear with me here)—and he needs to wear 8 pairs of socks on each of his 4 feet in order to make his running shoes stay on. (It's a giraffe thing.) How many total socks does he need?

Got that? OK- 4 giraffes are going jogging. They all need to wear 8 pairs on each of their 4 feet of socks to get their shoes to stay on. How many socks is it now?

Work It Out!

Jane loves giant chocolate chip cookies. Kirsten loves orange slices (the candy, obviously). Jane has tons of orange slices. Kirsten's dad makes giant chocolate chip cookies all the time. Jane has agreed to give Kirsten 5 orange slices for every giant cookie she brings on Mondays, Wednesdays and Fridays, and 6 orange slices for every cookie on Tuesdays and Thursdays. Use the IN/OUT machines below to determine how many orange slices Kirsten can expect depending on the number of cookies she brings in.

IN		OUT
4	5 orange slices	
5		
6		
7		
8		

IN		OUT
4	6 orange slices	
5		
6		
7		
8		

Build Your Skills!

Michael and Margot are building a couch fort in the living room. Calculate the area of the fort if they use blankets with the following dimensions.

4ft X 8ft =	5ft X 11ft =	5ft X 8ft =

You are kicking major math, kid!

Day 28

Use skip counting to fill in the multiplication matrix below. Did you notice we added 9's? We're up to 9's, Dr. Math!

	X 1	X 2	X 3	X 4	X 5	X 6	X 7	X 8	X 9	X 10	X 11	X 12
5:												
6:												
7:												
8:												
9:												

Work It Out!

Flip the script and find the missing factors in these multiplication matrices! Then complete them.

X			
	0		
		8	
			18

X			
	32		
		45	
			60

X			
	60		
		77	
			96

Fast Facts!

Its time for a 8's time test! Remember: Speed over correctness!

See if you can answer these 20 questions in under a minute!

8 X 6 =	8 X 1 =	8 X 5 =	8 X 11 =	10 X 8 =
8 X 4 =	7 X 8 =	9 X 8 =	8 X 8 =	2 X 8 =
8 X 8 =	3 X 8 =	6 X 8 =	12 X 8 =	4 X 8 =
5 X 8 =	8 X 2 =	1 X 8 =	8 X 3 =	7 X 8 =

Time: __________

Fun Alert: Bump!

Step 1: Draw a grid that is at least 4 by 8 squares- but you can really have as many as you want!

Step 2: Assign each square a number between 1 and 36. You can't use 7, 11, 13, 17, 19, 23, 26, 29, 31, 33 because it's impossible to roll the dice to get those numbers.

Play: The goal is to claim 4 squares in a row. To claim a square, roll the dice. You may place a token on the square that has product of the two numbers shown.

BUMP! If the product of your roll is already claimed by someone else, you can **bump** the other player's token. The token is taken completely off the table.

Good Stuff! Keep at it!

Day 29

Use Your Tools!

Stewart has requested a 8-tier strawberry birthday cake for his 8th birthday. He wants exactly 6 strawberries in each layer. How many strawberries will his mom need to make the cake? Use circle/dot to answer this question.

Stewart's mom has decided to decorate the cake with 8 sugar 8's on each of the 8 tiers. How many 8's will that be?

Fast Facts!

Write your 8's multiplication facts, fast as you can! 1-12. Don't forget to time yourself so you can track your progress!

8 X 1 = 8		
8 X 2 =		

Time: ___________

Multiplication Maze!

Cool Fact: Did you know that if you add the digits of any product of 9 , it always adds to 9? Let's try 1 or 2.

9 X 2 = 18   1 + 8 = 9

9 X 3 = 27   2 + 7 = 9

You try a few!

Keep it up, Math Miracle!

Day 30

Fast Facts!

Its time for a 8's time test!

See if you can answer these 20 questions in under a minute!

8 X 6 =	8 X 1 =	8 X 5 =	8 X 11 =	10 X 8 =
8 X 4 =	7 X 8 =	9 X 8 =	8 X 8 =	2 X 8 =
8 X 8 =	3 X 8 =	6 X 8 =	12 X 8 =	4 X 8 =
5 X 8 =	8 X 2 =	1 X 8 =	8 X 3 =	7 X 8 =

Time: ________

Work It Out!

Tommy has an enormous button collection. He is arranging his buttons in rows on trays of various sizes. Use arrays to calculate how many buttons are on the various trays below.

6 X 9 =	9 X 11 =	7 X 9=
9 X 3 =	9 X 2 =	9 X 12 =

Work It Out!

Bailey's parents have agreed to give her $8 for every time she rakes the yard and $9 for every time that she washes their two dogs. Use the IN/OUT machines to calculate how much money she can earn as she does more and more of her chores.

IN		OUT
2	$8 per	
3		
4		
5		
6		

IN		OUT
2	$9 per	
3		
4		
5		
6		

Use Your Tools!

Rhoda and Riley are building a castle out of twinkies! There are 6 towers and each tower is made from 9 layers of twinkie squares (4 twinkies for each layer). How many twinkies are there in each tower? How many twinkies are there total? Use arrays and the distributive property to answer this question.

Amazing work today, Math Royalty!

Day 31
Build Your Skills!

Use skip counting to fill in the open boxes of this multiplication matrix. Be careful near the cliff edges. Don't look down!

	X 1	X 2	X 3	X 4	X 5	X 6	X 7	X 8	X 9	X 10	X 11	X 12
6:												
7:												
8:												
9:												

Work It Out!

Fill in these backward matrices. No cheating, do the big numbers first!

X	12	11	10
9			
8			
7			

X	9	8	7
4			
3			
2			

X	10	9	8
7			
6			
5			

Fast Facts!

Write your 9's multiplication facts, fast as you can! 1-12. Don't forget to time yourself so you can track your progress!

9 X 1 = 9		
9 X 2 =		

Time: ___________

Use Your Tools!

Freddie has created a supply train out of several pairs of his father's shoes. Each train carries 9 of Freddie's army men. If Freddie uses 4 pairs of shoes, how many army men can he carry?

What if Freddie adds his mothers shoes? They can only carry 6 army men each but she has 9 pairs. How many army men can his mother's shoe train carry?

Wow, Great job! See you tomorrow, Math-inator!

Day 32

Build Your Skills!

Use skip counting to fill in the multiplication matrix. We're into double digits!

	X 1	X 2	X 3	X 4	X 5	X 6	X 7	X 8	X 9	X 10	X 11	X 12
6:												
7:												
8:												
9:												
10:												

Work It Out!

Find the missing factors in these multiplication matrices! 10s

X			
	80		
		99	
			120

X			
	70		
		88	
			108

X			
	28		
		40	
			54

Multiplication Maze!

Fast Facts!

Its time for a 9's time test!

See if you can answer these 20 questions in under a minute!

9 X 6 =	9 X 1 =	9 X 5 =	9 X 11 =	10 X 9 =
9 X 4 =	7 X 9 =	9 X 9 =	8 X 9 =	2 X 9 =
9 X 8 =	3 X 9 =	6 X 9 =	12 X 9 =	4 X 9 =
5 X 9 =	9 X 2 =	1 X 9 =	9 X 3 =	7 X 9 =

Time: ___________

Great Going Today!

Day 33

Work It Out!

Derek is making tropical punch for his soccer team party. But he's not sure how many people will show up or if he will run out of the big glasses. If each cup of powder makes 8 glasses of punch how much punch can he make? What if each cup of powder makes 9 glasses? Use the IN/OUT machines to help Derek figure it out!

IN	Big	OUT
8	8 cups	
9		
10		
11		
12		

IN	Small	OUT
8	9 cups	
9		
10		
11		
12		

Fast Facts!

Write your 10's multiplication facts, fast as you can! 1-12. Don't forget to time yourself so you can track your progress!

10 X 1 = 10		
10 X 2 =		

Time: ____________

Work It Out!

10 is a great number to use when working with the distributive function. Use distributive arrays and your 10's facts to calculate the products below.

3 X 16 =	4 X 18 =
2 X 13 =	4 X 15 =

Fun Alert: Multiplication War! Do you know the card game, War? In the multiplication version you just multiply the two cards together and whoever gets the answer first wins both cards! Jacks = 11; Queens = 12; Kings = 13; Ace = 1. Now, off to battle with you!

Keep it up, Math-Magician!

Day 34

Fast Facts!

Its time for a 9's time test! Remember, speed counts!
See if you can answer these 20 questions in under a minute!

9 X 6 =	9 X 1 =	9 X 5 =	9 X 11 =	10 X 9 =
9 X 4 =	7 X 9 =	9 X 9 =	8 X 9 =	2 X 9 =
9 X 8 =	3 X 9 =	6 X 9 =	12 X 9 =	4 X 9 =
5 X 9 =	9 X 2 =	1 X 9 =	9 X 3 =	7 X 9 =

Time: _________

Work It Out!

Fill in these backward matrices. No cheating, do the big numbers first!

X	7	6	5
12			
11			
10			

X	11	10	9
4			
3			
2			

X	10	9	8
9			
8			
7			

Use Your Tools!

James has dreamed himself into a real life video game. On this level he is jumping from one giant mushroom to the next. There are 5 feet between each mushroom. If James jumps to 11 mushrooms before completing the level, how many feet does he jump in total? Use arrays to answer this question.

On the next level, James has to collect rings that are on the legs of 3 enormous caterpillars. If each caterpillar has 16 legs, how many rings can James collect? Use the distributive function and your 10's facts to answer this question.

Finally, James must hit each lady bug on the head 7 times before he can win the game. If there are 12 lady bugs in his way, how many hits must he make before he can make his way to the winner's stand?

Wonderful work, Math Kid! Catch you later!

Day 35
Build Your Skills!

Use skip counting to fill in the multiplication matrix. We're into double digits!

	X 1	X 2	X 3	X 4	X 5	X 6	X 7	X 8	X 9	X 10	X 11	X 12
7:												
8:												
9:												
10:												
11:												

Work It Out!

Fill in the missing factors in these multiplication matrices!

X			
	90		
		110	
			132

X			
	32		
		45	
			60

X			
	14		
		24	
			36

Fast Facts!

Write your 11's multiplication facts, fast as you can! 1-12. Don't forget to time yourself so you can track your progress!

11 X 1 = 11		
11 X 2 =		

Time: ___________

Multiplication Maze!

Loving Your Progress!

Day 36

Fast Facts!

Its time for a 10's time test!

See if you can answer these 20 questions in under a minute!

10 X 6 =	*10 X 1 =*	*10 X 5 =*	*10 X 11 =*	*10 X 10 =*
10 X 4 =	*7 X 10 =*	*9 X 10 =*	*8 X 10 =*	*2 X 10 =*
10 X 8 =	*3 X 10 =*	*6 X 10 =*	*12 X 10 =*	*4 X 10 =*
5 X 10 =	*10 X 2 =*	*1 X 10 =*	*10 X 3 =*	*7 X 10 =*

Time: _________

Flex 'Em!

Rory is having a "bandit" birthday party and is creating disguises for all of his friends. Each bandit needs a mustache, a hat, a bandanna, and sunglasses. If Rory is having 11 people at his party, how many total items does he need to have for the disguises for his friends? You can use arrays or circle/Dot to answer this question.

Work It Out!

Cassy has decided to make homemade cinnamon raisin bread for the class picnic. She is trying to decide how many loafs she will need for 50 3rd graders. Cassy has figured out that the total number of slices from each loaf will be either 9 or 10. Use the IN/OUT machines to determine how many slices she will get out of different numbers of loafs if she gets 9 or 10 slices from each loaf.

IN		OUT
2	9 slices per loaf	
3		
4		
5		
6		

IN		OUT
2	10 slices per loaf	
3		
4		
5		
6		

Cool Fact: 11's trick! Do know about the 11's trick for numbers 2-9?

11 X 2 = 22
11 X 3 = 33
11 X 4 = 44

Notice anything?

Yep, that's right! For any number 2-9 when you multiply it by 11 you just list the same number again!

Something Encouraging!

Day 37

Fast Facts!

Write your 11's multiplication facts, fast as you can! 1-12. Don't forget to time yourself so you can track your progress!

11 X 1 = 11		
11 X 2 =		

Time: __________

Work It Out!

Elliot is going to surprise his parents by constructing a giant ant farm in their living room. He is choosing between several different designs and he needs to calculate how many square feet of space he will need for each. Use arrays to help Elliot calculate the square feet in each of the designs below.

6ft X 10ft =	**11ft X 11ft =**	**7ft X 6ft=**
9ft X 10ft =	**8ft X 6ft =**	**5ft X 12ft =**

Cool Fact: 11's past 10! For any number 10 and up, you just add the two digits of the number and stick the sum in between the original two digits.

So... 12 X 11 =

1 (1+2) 2

Try it!

12 X 11 = 1 3 2 = 132

Multiplication Maze!

		3	4	5	6	7	8	9	10	11	12	
	3											
	4											
Start!	5											
	6											End!
	7											
	8											
	9											
	10											
	11											

You did it again, Math Master!

Day 38

Fast Facts!

Its time for a 11's time test!

See if you can answer these 20 questions in under a minute!

11 X 6 =	11 X 1 =	11 X 5 =	11 X 11 =	11 X 10 =
11 X 4 =	7 X 11 =	9 X 11 =	8 X 11 =	2 X 11 =
11 X 8 =	3 X 11 =	6 X 11 =	12 X 11 =	4 X 11 =
5 X 11 =	11 X 2 =	1 X 11 =	11 X 3 =	7 X 11 =

Time: ________

Build Your Skills!

Fill in the open boxes on this multiplication matrix. Don't step on the crack or you'll... explode into a million pieces! Uhh, that's not it, is it?

	X 1	X 2	X 3	X 4	X 5	X 6	X 7	X 8	X 9	X 10	X 11	X 12
7:												
8:												
9:												
10:												
11:												

Work It Out!

Fill in the missing factors in these multiplication matrices!

X			
	90		
		110	
			132

X			
	40		
		55	
			72

X			
	72		
		90	
			110

Use Your Tools!

Alecia has gotten a pogo-stick for her birthday. (Look it up if you don't know about this awesomeness!) She is having a race with her friend Aaron. With every jump Alecia goes 9 feet. With every jump Aaron goes 7 feet. How many feet will Alecia have travelled in 10 jumps? How many feet will Aaron have travelled in 10 jumps?

Wow!

Day 39
Build Your Skills!

Use skip counting to fill in the open boxes of this multiplication matrix. Be Careful! Someone told me that there is lava in the black squares!

	X 1	X 2	X 3	X 4	X 5	X 6	X 7	X 8	X 9	X 10	X 11	X 12
8:												
9:												
10:												
11:												
12:												

Fast Facts!

Write your 12's multiplication facts, fast as you can! 1-12. Don't forget to time yourself so you can track your progress!

12 X 1 = 12		
12 X 2 =		

Time: ___________

Use Your Tools!

Danny and DeShawn are playing hedgehog invaders. To play the game they must construct defences around their territory against the horrible hedgehog army. How many square feet will they have to protect if their territory has the following dimensions?

6 X 12 =	9 X 12 =	7 X 12=
12 X 3 =	12 X 2 =	12 X 12 =

Work It Out!

Fill in these backward matrices. Remember, do the big numbers first!

X	12	11	10
12			
11			
10			

X	12	11	10
4			
3			
2			

X	12	11	10
9			
8			
7			

Great going today, Math-Magician!

Day 40

Fast Facts!

It's time for a 11's time test! Remember the need for speed!

See if you can answer these 20 questions in under a minute!

11 X 6 =	11 X 1 =	11 X 5 =	11 X 11 =	11 X 10 =
11 X 4 =	7 X 11 =	9 X 11 =	8 X 11 =	2 X 11 =
11 X 8 =	3 X 11 =	6 X 11 =	12 X 11 =	4 X 11 =
5 X 11 =	11 X 2 =	1 X 11 =	11 X 3 =	7 X 11 =

Time: ________

Work It Out!

Mariah is trying to calculate how much face-paint she needs for her sleep over (so that she and her friends can paint themselves as night owls, duh!). But she is not sure how many friends will come over- 4, 5 or 6- or how many stars she should paint on each of their faces (because feathers would be weird, duh!)

Use the IN/OUT machine to find out how many stars will be painted if she paints 11 or 12 starts on each of her friends faces.

IN		OUT
4	11 stars per face	
5		
6		

IN		OUT
4	12 stars per face	
5		
6		

Giant Multiplication Maze!

		1	2	3	4	5	6	7	8	9	10	
Start	0											
	1											
	2											
	3											
	4											
	5											
	6											
	7											
	8											
	9											
	10											
	11											End
	12											

Way to math another day, Math-inator!

Day 41

Fast Facts!

Write your 12's multiplication facts, fast as you can! 1-12. Don't forget to time yourself so you can track your progress!

12 X 1 = 12		
12 X 2 =		

Time: ___________

Work It Out!

Bernard is preparing the hot chocolate for his 4th grade class's Christmas party. He has divided the class into groups based on how many marshmallows they want. How many marshmallows will he need for each group?

4 cups X 12 mm's =	**9 cups X 7 mm's =**	**5 cups X 10 mm's=**
12 cups X 3 mm's=	**8 cups X 9 mm's =**	**11 cups X 11 mm =**

Use Your Tools!

Reni and Rooster are next-door neighbours. They have set up an obstacle course that goes around both of their front and back yards. The course requires exactly 16 jumps, 22 stretches, 5 tip-toes, and 11 swings to complete it. If Reni and Rooster invite their friends Myra and Maddy to attempt the course with them, how many tip-toes will need to be completed by all 4 of the kids?

How many stretches will be conducted if all 4 kids run the obstacle course? Use the distributive function to answer this question.

Finally, how many swings will there be if Myra goes home but Maddy, Reni, and Rooster complete the course 1 more time?

Absolutely fantastic work today!

Day 42

Fast Facts!

Its time for a 12's time test!

See if you can answer these 20 questions in under a minute!

12 X 6 =	*12 X 1 =*	*12 X 5 =*	*12 X 11 =*	*12 X 10 =*
12 X 4 =	*7 X 12 =*	*9 X 12 =*	*8 X 12 =*	*2 X 12 =*
12 X 8 =	*3 X 12 =*	*6 X 12 =*	*12 X 12 =*	*4 X 12 =*
5 X 12 =	*12 X 2 =*	*1 X 12 =*	*12 X 3 =*	*7 X 12 =*

Time: __________

Work It Out!

Having had enough of Zorbo's nonsense, President Earnest World has gotten a cloning machine of his own. He plan is to create enough nuts that when Zorbo's squirrel army arrives, they will be too distracted with eating to attack anyone. Use the IN/OUT machines to determine how many nuts President World can create with the dial set to 11 or 12.

IN		OUT
8	Dial Set to 11	
9		
10		
11		
12		

IN		OUT
8	Dial Set to 12	
9		
10		
11		
12		

Build Your Skills!

Fill in the missing factors in these multiplication matrices!

X			
	100		
		121	
			144

X			
	42		
		56	
			72

X			
	90		
		110	
			132

Use Your Tools!

Did you know that bamboo can grow up to 15 inches per day? Emma has a garden with 10 bamboo shoots in it, how many inches of bamboo will grow every day?

What if she has 100 bamboo shoots? How many inches of bamboo will grow each day now?

Impressive work today, Math Maniac! See you tomorrow!

Day 43

Work It Out!

Zena has a small menagerie of animals: with 6 monkeys, 9 bears, 8 swans, 7 zebras, 11 antelopes, and 12 aligators. They are all going to the beach. She needs to order 1 pair of sunglass for each animal in each group. Calculate how many pairs of sunglasses she needs for each animal below.

6 X 6 =	9 X 9 =	8 X 8=
7 X 7 =	11 X 11 =	12 X 12 =

Fast Facts!

Write your doubles multiplication facts, fast as you can! 1-12. Don't forget to time yourself so you can track your progress!

1 X 1 = 1		
2 X 2 =		

Time: ___________

Giant Multiplication Maze!

		1	2	3	4	5	6	7	8	9	10	
	0											
	1											
Start!	2											
	3											
	4											
	5											
	6											
	7											
	8											End!
	9											
	10											
	11											
	12											

Wow, what a day! Great work, Dr. Math!

Day 44

Lets Learn Something!

Today we will learn how to multiply by 1 million! Or 1 zillion, even! Here's the trick. You can multiply any number ending in zeros by first taking the zero's off, multiply the numbers, and then add all the zeros on to the end of the product. So...

3 X 400=

3 X 4 = 12

Add back in the zeros: 1200

You can do it with any number. Try 4 X 2,000,000 (that's 2 million!)

4 X 2 = 8

Add back in the 6 zeros: 8,000,000!

Fast Facts!

Write your 100's multiplication facts, fast as you can! 1-12. You can do 1000's if you want! ;) Don't forget to time yourself so you can track your progress!

1 X 100 = 100		
2 X 100 =		

Time: ___________

Work It Out!

Fill in the missing factors in these multiplication matrices!

X			
	25		
		36	
			49

X			
	100		
		121	
			144

X			
	49		
		64	
			81

Use Your Tools!

Zorbo has designed mech-suits for his squirrel army. Each suit requires 500 tiny pieces of metal and over 6000 gears! If Zorbo has 5000 squirrels in the army, how many gears will he need? How many pieces of metal? Use the distributive function and what you know about multiplying numbers ending in zero to answer this question.

Amazing job, Mathosaurus Rex!

Day 45

Cool Fact: This our last day together. Can you believe it?! You have done some amazing work over these last few months! And I have a super fun last day for you.

Starting with the best cool fact I know! Here it is.

You have done some pretty big multiplication problems over the last 45 days. So big, that if someone had told 1st grade you that you would be doing 6000 X 4500... - 1st grade you probably wouldn't believe them!

Think about what that means! You have abilities that you can't even imagine. And they are just waiting to come out with some hard work and practice!

So, work hard and have fun, rowdy kid!
You never know what you'll be able to do tomorrow!

Fast Facts!

Its time for a time test!

See if you can answer these 20 questions in under a minute!

12 X 6 =	*12 X 1 =*	*12 X 5 =*	*12 X 11 =*	*12 X 10 =*
12 X 4 =	*7 X 12 =*	*9 X 12 =*	*8 X 12 =*	*2 X 12 =*
12 X 8 =	*3 X 12 =*	*6 X 12 =*	*12 X 12 =*	*4 X 12 =*
5 X 12 =	*12 X 2 =*	*1 X 12 =*	*12 X 3 =*	*7 X 12 =*

Time: ___________

Multiplication Maze!

Use Your Tools!

President World needs your help! He needs 20,000 kids to do 200 multiplication problems each so that he can win a bet with his arch nemesis Emperor Zorbo from planet Mathos. How many multiplication problems would that be?

(Psst: If you have completed this book, you have done over 2000 multiplication problems, Math Star!)

Way to Finish Strong, Rowdy Math Master!

Answer Key

Day 1

Work It Out!

2 X 3 = ? *2+2+2 = 6*	**3 X 6 =** *3+3+3+3+3+3=18*	**2 X 9 =** *2+2+2+2+2+2+2+2+2= 18*
3 X 12 = *3+3+3+3+3+3+3+3+3+3+3+3= 36*	**2 X 5 =** *2+2+2+2+2= 10*	**3 X 2 =** *3+3=6*
3 X 3 = *3+3+3=9*	**1 X 11 =** *11*	**3 X 4 =** *3+3+3+3=12*
2 X 7 = *2+2+2+2+2+2+2= 14*	**1 X 8 =** *8*	**3 X 10 =** *3+3+3+3+3+3+3+3+3+3= 30*

Build Your Skill!

2's: 2, 4, 6, 8, 10, 12, 14, 16, 18, 20, 22, 24

3's: 3, 6, 9, 12, 15, 18, 21, 24, 27, 30, 33, 36

Day 2

Use Your Tools!

The school roller skating night is in 3 weeks...

$4 X 3 weeks = $12

Build Your Skills!

Skip counting 2's

2's: 2, 4, 6, 8, 10, 12, 14, 16, 18, 20, 22, 24

	X 1	X 2	X 3	X 4	X 5	X 6	X 7	X 8	X 9	X 10	X 11	X 12
2:	2	4	6	8	10	12	14	16	18	20	22	24

Work It Out!

2 X 4 =	3 X 7 =	2 X 10 =
2+2+2+2=8	3+3+3+3+3+3+3=21	2+2+2+2+2+2+2+2+2+2= 20
2 X 12 =	**3 X 5 =**	**2 X 2 =**
2+2+2+2+2+2+2+2+2+2+2+2= 24	3+3+3+3+3= 15	2+2= 4
3 X 6 =	**1 X 10 =**	**3 X 8 =**
3+3+3+3+3+3= 18	10	3+3+3+3+3+3+3+3= 24
3 X 7 =	**2 X 8 =**	**9 X 3 =**
3+3+3+3+3+3+3= 21	2+2+2+2+2+2+2+2= 16	3+3+3+3+3+3+3+3+3= 27

Fast Facts!

2 X 1 = 2	2 X 5 = 10	2 X 9 = 18
2 X 2 = 4	2 X 6 = 12	2 X 10 = 20
2 X 3 = 6	2 X 7 = 14	2 X 11 = 22
2 X 4 = 8	2 X 8 = 16	2 X 12 = 24

Day 3

Warm-Up!

	X 1	X 2	X 3	X 4	X 5	X 6	X 7	X 8	X 9	X 10	X 11	X 12
2:	2	4	6	8	10	12	14	16	18	20	22	24
3:	3	6	9	12	15	18	21	24	27	30	33	36

Work It Out!

Daredevil Park is the best park in town! It has 4 Merry-Go-Rounds! If 5 kids can fit on each Merry-Go-Round, how many kids can play on Merry-Go-Rounds at one time? Use the circle/dot method!

4 merry-go-rounds X 5 kids = 20 kids

Fast Facts!

2 X 1 = 2	*2 X 5 = 10*	*2 X 9 = 18*
2 X 2 = 4	*2 X 6 = 12*	*2 X 10 = 20*
2 X 3 = 6	*2 X 7 = 14*	*2 X 11 = 22*
2 X 4 = 8	*2 X 8 = 16*	*2 X 12 = 24*

Build Your Skill!

3 X 9 = 27	2 X 11 = 22
3 X 12 = 36	2 X 9 = 18

Day 4

	X 1	X 2	X 3	X 4	X 5	X 6	X 7	X 8	X 9	X 10	X 11	X 12
2:	2	4	6	8	10	12	14	16	18	20	22	24
4:	4	8	12	16	20	24	28	32	36	40	44	48

Fast Facts!

2 X 6= 12	2 X 8 = 16	2 X 9 = 18
2 X 2 = 4	2 X 4 = 8	2 X 5 = 10
2 X 5 = 10	2 X 12 = 24	2 X 7 = 14
2 X 3 = 6	2 X 1 = 2	2 X 8 = 16
2 X 7 = 21	2 X 3 = 6	2 X 4 = 8
2 X 9 = 18	2 X 6 = 12	2 X 12 = 24
2 X 10 = 20	2 X 11 = 22	FINISHED!

Use Your Tools!

Zorbo and his cloning machine

IN		OUT
2	Dial Shows 2X.....	*4*
3		*6*
4		*8*
5		*10*
6		*12*

IN		OUT
3	Dial Shows 3X.....	9
4		12
5		15
6		18
7		21

IN		OUT
2	Dial Shows 4X.....	8
3		12
4		16
5		20
6		24

IN		OUT
8	Dial Shows 3X.....	24
9		27
10		30
11		33
12		36

Day 5

Build Your Skills!

2	2	3	4
2	4	6	8
3	6	9	12
4	8	12	16

X	8	9	10
2	16	18	20
3	24	27	30
4	32	36	40

X	5	6	7
2	10	12	14
3	15	18	21
4	20	24	28

Fast Facts!

3 X 1 = 3	*3 X 5= 15*	*3 X 9 = 27*
3 X 2 = 6	*3 X 6 = 18*	*3 X 10 = 30*
3 X 3 = 9	*3 X 7 = 21*	*3 X 11 = 33*
3 X 4 = 12	*3 X 8 = 24*	*3 X 12 = 36*

Day 6

Work It Out!

2 X 4 = *8*	3 X 7 = 21	12 X 3 = 36
7 X 3 = 21	3 X 5 = 15	3 X 9 = 27
3 X 6 = 18	3 X 12 = 36	4 X 2 = 8
5 X 3 = 15	6 X 3 = 18	9 X 3 = 27

Fast Facts!

3 X 1 = 3	*3 X 5= 15*	*3 X 9 = 27*
3 X 2 = 6	*3 X 6 = 18*	*3 X 10 = 30*
3 X 3 = 9	*3 X 7 = 21*	*3 X 11 = 33*
3 X 4 = 12	*3 X 8 = 24*	*3 X 12 = 36*

Use Your Tools!

Morris and Molly and peanut butter crackers

6 sandwiches; 2 crackers per sandwich = 6 X 2 = 12

Day 7

Warm It Up!

	X 1	X 2	X 3	X 4	X 5	X 6	X 7	X 8	X 9	X 10	X 11	X 12
2:	2	4	6	8	10	12	14	16	18	20	22	24
3:	3	6	9	12	15	18	21	24	27	30	33	36
4:	4	8	12	16	20	24	28	32	36	40	44	48
5:	5	10	15	20	25	30	35	40	45	50	55	60

Work It Out!

1. Owen has adjusted his water balloon so that it now bounces 3 spaces each time. If balloon bounces 4 times, how many spaces will it go?

3 spaces X 4 bounces = 12 spaces

2. Unfortunately, Owen's little brother, Orion, got a hold of the cannon. Now any balloon that is shot out of there goes 11 spaces with each bounce but it can only bounce 2 times. How far will the water balloon travel?

11 spaces X 2 bounces = 22 spaces

Fast Facts!

3 X 5 = 15	3 X 12 = 36	3 X 7 = 21	3 X 10 = 30	9 X 3 = 27
3 X 3 = 9	3 X 1 = 3	8 X 3 = 24	5 X 3 = 15	1 X 3 = 3
7 X 3 = 21	2 X 3 = 6	3 X 4 = 12	11 X 3 = 33	6 X 3 = 18
3 X 9 = 27	3 X 6 = 18	12 X 3 = 36	3 X 2 = 6	3 X 8 = 24

Day 8

Work It Out!

5 X 4 = 20	3 X 7 = 21	10 X 4 = 40
4 X 3 = 12	4 X 3 = 36	5 X 11 = 55
3 X 6 = 18	4 X 4 = 16	4 X 12 = 48

Build Your Skills!

X	0	1	2
2	0	2	4
3	0	3	6
4	0	4	8

X	3	4	5
3	9	12	15
4	12	16	20
5	15	20	25

X	5	6	7
3	15	18	21
4	20	24	28
5	25	30	35

Flex 'Em!

Penny and the coffee cup.

3 bounces X 6 ft = 18 ft

Day 9

Build Your Skills!

	X 1	X 2	X 3	X 4	X 5	X 6	X 7	X 8	X 9	X 10	X 11	X 12
2:					10	12	14	16	18			24
3:				12	15	18	21	24			33	36
4:			12	16	20	24	28			40	44	48
5:		10	15	20	25	30			45	50	55	60

Jack is selling candy bars ...

$1 per candy bar X 8 candy bars = $8 per box

4 boxes X $8 = $32

Jack does NOT have enough money yet.

Fast Facts!

4 X 1 = 4	4 X 5 = 20	4 X 9 =36
4 X 2 =8	4 X 6 = 24	4 X 10 =40
4 X 3 = 12	4 X 7 = 28	4 X 11 = 44
4 X 4 = 16	4 X 8 = 32	4 X 12 = 48

Work It Out!

5 X 6 = 30	**3 X 4 = 12**	**12 X 4 = 48**
7 X 5 = 35	**2 X 5 = 10**	**3 X 9 = 27**
5 X 8 = 40	**3 X 11 = 33**	**5 X 7 = 35**

Day 10

Fast Facts!

3 X 5 = 15	3 X 12 = 36	3 X 7 = 21	3 X 10 = 30	9 X 3 = 27
3 X 3 = 9	3 X 1 = 3	8 X 3 = 24	5 X 3 = 15	1 X 3 = 3
7 X 3 = 21	2 X 3 = 6	3 X 4 = 12	11 X 3 = 33	6 X 3 = 18
3 X 9 = 27	3 X 6 = 18	12 X 3 = 36	3 X 2 = 6	3 X 8 = 24

Work It Out!

Jenny is selling friendship bracelets for $1 each...

IN		OUT
2	$3 per bracelet	6
3		9
4		12
5		15
6		18

IN		OUT
2	$4 per bracelet	8
3		12
4		16
5		20
6		24

Use Your Tools!

Billy and Booster are ...

Each robot can only travel 4 feet. How far will 4 robots get them? How many different ways can you think to solve this problem?

4 robots X 4 feet = 16 feet

Booster spends the morning upgrading the robots so that they can travel 6 feet in one run. Now, how far can 4 robots get them?

4 robots X 6 feet = 24 feet

The robots can bring 5 cups of popcorn per trip. If they make 7 trips, how much popcorn do Billy and Booster get to eat?

5 cups X 7 trips = 35 cups

Day 11

Warm It Up!

	X 1	X 2	X 3	X 4	X 5	X 6	X 7	X 8	X 9	X 10	X 11	X 12
3:	3	6	9	12	15	18	21	24	27	30	33	36
4:	4	8	12	16	20	24	28	32	36	40	44	48
5:	5	10	15	20	25	30	35	40	45	50	55	60
6:	6	12	18	24	30	36	42	48	54	60	66	72

Use Your Tools!

Lily is planning a surprise...

If there are 5 sisters in total and they each shoot off 6 firecrackers, how many firecrackers will there be?

5 sisters X 6 firecrackers = 30 firecrackers

Build Your Skills!

X	0	1	2
3	0	3	6
4	0	4	8
5	0	5	10

X	3	4	5
4	12	16	20
5	15	20	25
6	18	24	30

X	6	7	8
4	24	28	32
5	30	35	40
6	36	42	48

X	0	1	2
0	0	0	0
1	0	1	2
2	0	2	4

X	9	10	11
3	27	30	33
4	36	40	44
5	45	50	55

X	10	11	12
4	40	44	48
5	50	55	60
6	60	66	72

Fast Facts!

4 X 1 = 4	4 X 5 = 20	4 X 9 =36
4 X 2 =8	4 X 6 = 24	4 X 10 =40
4 X 3 = 12	4 X 7 = 28	4 X 11 = 44
4 X 4 = 16	4 X 8 = 32	4 X 12 = 48

Day 12

Fast Facts!

4 X 5 = 20	4 X 12 = 48	3 X 4 = 12	4 X 10 = 40	9 X 4 = 36
4 X 3 = 12	4 X 7 = 28	8 X 4 = 32	5 X 4 = 20	1 X 4 = 4
7 X 4 = 28	2 X 4 = 8	3 X 4 = 12	11 X 4 = 44	6 X 4 = 24
4 X 4 = 16	4 X 6 = 24	12 X 4 = 48	4 X 2 = 8	4 X 8 = 32

Build Your Skills!

	X 1	X 2	X 3	X 4	X 5	X 6	X 7	X 8	X 9	X 10	X 11	X 12
3:			9	12	15	18				30	33	36
4:	4			16	20			32			44	48
5:	5	10					35	40	45			60
6:	6	12	18	24	30	36	42	48	54	60	66	72

Work It Out!

Olly won the lottery and with his winnings he bought an entire truck full of foot-long bubble gum...

5 X 6 = 30 feet of gum for Miles	6 X 4 = 24 feet of gum for Betsy	12 X 6 = 72 feet of gum for Asher
6 X 5 = 30 feet of gum for Malik	2 X 6 = 12 feet of gum for Jaden	6 X 9 = 54 feet of gum for Belle
6 X 8 = 48 feet of gum for Emma	6 X 11 = 66 feet of gum for Drew	6 X 7 = 42 feet of gum for Henry

Day 13

Use Your Tools!

Samantha is having a scavenger hunt birthday party...

9 friends X 3 scoops = 27 scoops

Giant marbles. At the beginning of the game each of the 9 girls starts with 5 "marbles." How many marbles are there?

9 girls X 5 marbles = 45 marbles

As a party gift Samantha gave each of her 8 friends 6 tadpoles! If all goes well in a few weeks there will be how many frogs hopping all around?

8 friends X 6 tadpoles = 48 tadpoles

Fast Facts!

4 X 7 = 28	*4 X 2 = 8*	*5 X 4 = 20*	*4 X 12 = 48*	*11 X 4 = 44*
4 X 5 = 20	*4 X 9 = 36*	*10 X 4 =40*	*7 X 4 = 28*	*3 X 4 = 12*
9 X 4 = 36	*4 X 4 = 16*	*4 X 4 = 16*	*1 X 4 = 4*	*8 X 4 = 32*
6 X 4 = 24	*4 X 8 = 32*	*12 X 4 = 48*	*4 X 4 = 16*	*4 X 10 = 40*

Build Your Skills!

	X 1	X 2	X 3	X 4	X 5	X 6	X 7	X 8	X 9	X 10	X 11	X 12
2:					10	12	14	16	18			24
3:				12	15	18	21	24			33	36
4:			`12	16	20	24	28			40	44	48
5:		10	15	20	25	30			45	50	55	60
6:	6	12	18	24	30			48	54	60	66	72

Day 14

Fast Facts!

5 X 1 = 5	5 X 5 = 25	5 X 9 = 45
5 X 2 = 10	5 X 6 = 30	5 X 10 = 50
5 X 3 = 15	5 X 7 = 35	5 X 11 = 55
5 X 4 = 20	5 X 8 = 40	5 X 12 = 60

Work It Out!

Alton is trying to predict how much money he will make from selling his super-awesome lemonade...

IN		OUT
2	$5 per cup	10
3		15
4		20
5		25
6		30

IN		OUT
2	$6 per cup	12
3		18
4		24
5		30
6		36

Flex 'Em!

Ricky is entering his pet rabbit, Fluffers, in the county bunny race. The race course is 20 feet long. At the start of training Fluffers travelled 2 feet with every jump. How many jumps did it take Fluffers to reach the end of the course? Use the number line to answer this question.

2 feet X ? jumps = 20 feet

2 X 10 = 20

10 jumps

Ricky's creative training program has doubled Fluffers the length of each of Fluffers' jumps 4 feet. Now how many jumps does it take for Fluffers to reach the finish line?

4 feet X ? jumps = 20 feet

4 X 5 = 20

5 jumps

Day 15

Work It Out!

6 X 6 = 36	**6 X 11 = 66**	**6 X 8 = 48**
6 X 3 = 18	**6 X 2 = 12**	**6 X 12 = 72**
6 X 9 = 54	**6 X 4 = 24**	**6 X 7 = 42**

Fast Facts!

4 X 6 =24	4 X 1 =4	4 X 4 =16	4 X 11 =44	10 X 4 =40
4 X 4 =16	4 X 8 =32	9 X 4 =36	6 X 4 = 24	2 X 4 =8
8 X 4 =32	3 X 4 =12	4 X 5 =20	12 X 4 =48	7 X 4 =28
5 X 4 =20	4 X 7 =28	1 X 4 =4	4 X 3 = 12	4 X 9 =36

Use Your Tools!

Peter Piper picked a peck of pickled peppers...

6 pecks X 12 peppers = 72 peppers

Build Your Skills!

X	4	5	6
4	16	20	24
5	20	25	30
6	24	30	36

X	4	5	6
10	40	50	60
11	44	55	66
12	48	60	72

X	4	5	6
7	28	35	42
8	32	40	48
9	36	45	54

Fast Facts!

5 X 1 = 5	5 X 5 = 25	5 X 9= 45
5 X 2 = 10	5 X 6 =30	5 X 10 =50
5 X 3 = 15	5 X 7 = 35	5 X 11 = 55
5 X 4=20	5 X 8 = 40	5 X 12 = 60

Use Your Tools!

Maya and Marion each have one pair of skates. If they can balance 5 cups on each skate, how may cups can they bring in one trip?

2 pairs = 4 skates

4 skates X 5 cups = 20 cups

If they can balance only 3 cups on each hand, how many cups can they bring in one trip. Use arrays to answer this question.

2 kids = 4 hands

4 hands X 3 cups = 12 cups

Day 17

Fast Facts!

6 X 1 = 6	*6 X 5 = 30*	*6 X 9 = 54*
6 X 2 = 12	*6 X 6 = 36*	*6 X 10 = 60*
6 X 3 = 18	*6 X 7 = 42*	*6 X 11 = 66*
6 X 4 = 24	*6 X 8 = 48*	*6 X 12 = 72*

Work It Out!

Esther's parents have made her a deal...

IN	socks	OUT
8	5 jelly beans	40
9		45
10		50
11		55
12		60

IN	Legos	OUT
8	6 jelly beans	48
9		54
10		60
11		66
12		72

Build Your Skills!

Use skip-counting to fill in the matrix below.

	X 2	X 3	X 4	X 5	X 6	X 7	X 8	X 9	X 10	X 11	X 12
0:	0	0	0	0	0	0	0	0	0	0	0
1:	2	3	4	5	6	7	8	9	10	11	12
2:	4	6	8	10	12	14	16	18	20	22	24
3:	6	9	12	15	18	21	24	27	30	33	36
4:	8	12	16	20	24	28	32	36	40	44	48
5:	10	15	20	25	30	35	40	45	50	55	60
6:	12	18	24	30	36	42	48	54	60	66	72
7:	14	21	28	35	42	49	56	63	70	77	84

Day 18

Multiplication Maze!

		1	2	3	4	5	6	7	8	9	10	
	0							0	0	0		
	1			3	4	5	6	7		9		
Start!	**2**	2	4			10				18		
	3		6		12	15			24	27		
	4		8		16				32		40	**End!**
	5		10	15	20				40	45	50	
	6		12									

Fast Facts!

5 X 6 = 30	*5 X 1 =5*	*5 X 5 = 25*	*5 X 11 = 55*	*10 X 5 = 50*
5 X 4 = 20	*5 X 8 = 40*	*9 X 5 = 45*	*6 X 5 = 30*	*2 X 5 = 10*
8 X 5 = 40	*3 X 5 = 15*	*6 X 5 = 30*	*12 X 5 = 60*	*7 X 5 = 35*
5 X 5 = 25	*5 X 7 = 35*	*1 X 5 = 5*	*5 X 3 = 15*	*5 X 9 =45*

Day 19

Fast Facts!

6 X 1 = 6	*6 X 5 = 30*	*6 X 9 = 54*
6 X 2 = 12	*6 X 6 = 36*	*6 X 10 = 60*
6 X 3 = 18	*6 X 7 = 42*	*6 X 11 = 66*
6 X 4 = 24	*6 X 8 = 48*	*6 X 12 = 72*

Work It Out!

Morris and Stacey are arguing over the perfect size for a guinea pig cage.

6ft X 7ft **42**	**7ft X 11ft** **77**	**7ft X 8ft** **56**
7ft X 3ft **21**	**7ft X 2ft** **14**	**7ft X 12ft** **84**

Build Your Skills!

X	**5**	**6**	**7**
4	20	24	28
5	25	30	35
6	30	36	42

X	**5**	**6**	**7**
10	50	60	70
11	55	66	77
12	60	72	84

X	**5**	**6**	**7**
7	35	40	45
8	42	48	54
9	49	56	63

Flex 'Em!

Jonas's mother claims that every square foot of his bed is completely covered in stuffed animals...

3 ft X 7 ft = 21 square feet

Day 20

Work It Out!

X	0	1	2
7	0	7	14
8	0	8	16
9	0	9	18

X	9	10	11
4	36	40	44
5	45	50	55
6	54	60	66

X	10	11	12
10	100	110	120
11	110	121	132
12	120	132	144

X	2	3	4
0	0	0	0
1	2	3	4
2	4	6	8

X	3	4	5
2	6	8	10
3	9	12	15
4	12	16	20

X	6	7	8
6	36	42	48
7	42	49	56
8	48	56	64

Fast Facts!

6 X 6 = 36	6 X 1 = 6	6 X 5 = 30	6 X 11 = 66	10 X 6 = 60
6 X 4 = 24	6 X 8 = 48	9 X 6 = 54	6 X 8 = 48	2 X 6 = 12
8 X 6 = 48	3 X 6 = 18	6 X 6 = 36	12 X 6 =72	7 X 6 = 42
5 X 6 = 30	6 X 7 = 42	1 X 6 = 6	6 X 3 = 18	6 X 9 = 54

U
se

Your Tools!

Micah and his family are at the beach...

6 ft X 12 ft = 72 square feet

Day 21

Fast Facts!

7 X 1 = 7	7 X 5 = 35	7 X 9 =63
7 X 2 = 14	7 X 6 = 42	7 X 10 = 70
7 X 3 = 21	7 X 7 = 49	7 X 11 = 77
7 X 4 = 28	7 X 8 - 56	7 X 12 = 84

Work It Out!

IN		OUT

3	7 minutes	21
4		28
5		35
6		42
7		49

IN		OUT
3	8 minutes	24
4		32
5		40
6		48
7		56

Multiplication Maze!

Use Your Tools!

Kristi's dog Bruno collects socks and hides them under one of his 3 dog beds.

		1	2	3	4	5	6	7	8	9	10	
	1			3	4	5				9		
	2					10	12	14	16	18		
Start!	3	3	6	9		15		21				
	4			12		20		28		36	40	**End!**
	5		10	15		25		35	40	45		
	6		12			30			48			
	7	7	14	21	28	35			56			

If there are 12 socks under each bed...

12 socks X 3 beds = 36 socks or

10 socks X 3 beds = 30 and 2 socks X 3 beds = 6

30 + 6 = 36

Day 22

Build Your Skills!

Fast Facts!

6 X 6 = 36	*6 X 1 =6*	*6 X 5 = 30*	*6 X 11 = 66*	*10 X 6 = 60*

	X 1	**X 2**	**X 3**	**X 4**	**X 5**	**X 6**	**X 7**	**X 8**	**X 9**	**X 10**	**X 11**	**X 12**
3:					15	18	21	24	27			36
4:				16	20	24	28	32			44	48
5:			15	20	25	30	35			50	55	60
6:		12	18	24	30	36			54	60	66	72
7:	7	14	21	28	35			56	63	70	77	84

6 X 4 = 24	*6 X 8 = 48*	*9 X 6 = 54*	*6 X 8 = 48*	*2 X 6 = 12*
8 X 6 = 48	*3 X 6 = 18*	*6 X 6 = 36*	*12 X 6 = 72*	*7 X 6 = 42*
5 X 6 = 30	*6 X 7 = 42*	*1 X 6 = 6*	*6 X 3 = 18*	*6 X 9 = 54*

Use Your Tools!

Anthony and Stella are preparing for the summer block-party...

3 ft X 10 ft = 30 square ft

A jumbo human bowling lane is 6ft wide and 24ft...

24 = 10 + 10 + 4

6 X 10 = 60

6 X 10 = 60

6 X 4 = 24

60 + 60 + 24 = 144 square feet

Day 23

Fast Facts!

7 X 1 = 7	*7 X 5 = 35*	*7 X 9 =63*
7 X 2 = 14	*7 X 6 = 42*	*7 X 10 = 70*
7 X 3 = 21	*7 X 7 = 49*	*7 X 11 = 77*
7 X 4 = 28	*7 X 8 - 56*	*7 X 12 = 84*

Work It Out!

Day 24

X	6	7	8
4	24	28	32
5	30	35	40
6	36	42	48

X	9	10	11
5	45	50	55
6	54	60	66
7	63	70	77

X	6	7	8
2	12	14	16
3	18	21	24
4	24	28	32

Build Your Skills!

Work It Out!

	X 1	X 2	X 3	X 4	X 5	X 6	X 7	X 8	X 9	X 10	X 11	X 12
6:	6	12	18	24	30	36	42	48	54	60	66	72
7:	7	14	21	28	35	42	49	56	63	70	77	84
8:	8	16	24	32	40	48	56	64	72	80	88	96

8 X 6 = **48**	**8 X 11 =** **88**
8 X 9 = **72**	**8 X 12 =** **96**

Fast Facts!

7 X 6 = 42	*7 X 1 = 7*	*7 X 5 = 35*	*7 X 11 = 77*	*10 X 7 = 70*
7 X 4 = 28	*7 X 8 = 56*	*9 X 7 = 63*	*7 X 8 = 56*	*2 X 7 = 14*
8 X 7 = 56	*3 X 7 = 21*	*6 X 7 = 42*	*12 X 7 = 84*	*7 X 7 = 49*
5 X 7 = 35	*7 X 7 = 49*	*1 X 7 = 7*	*7 X 3 = 21*	*7 X 9 = 63*

Day 25

Build Your Skills!

	1	2	3	4	5	6	7	8	9	10	11	12
5:			15	20	25	30				50	55	60
6:	6			24	30			48			66	72
7:	7	14					49	56	63			84
8:	8	16	24	32	40	48	56	64	72	80	88	96

Work It Out!

Alaster is working on his basketball skills...

4 X 8 =	6 X 11 =	7 X 9 =
32	66	63

Fast Facts!

8 X 1 = 8	*8 X 5 = 40*	*8 X 9 = 72*
8 X 2 = 16	*8 X 6 = 48*	*8 X 10 = 80*
8 X 3 = 24	*8 X 7 = 56*	*8 X 11 = 88*
8 X 4 = 32	*8 X 8 =64*	*8 X 12 = 96*

Work It Out!

Zorbo is back with his cloning machine!

IN		OUT
8	Dial at 7	56
9		63
10		70
11		77
12		84

IN		OUT
8	Dial at 8	64
9		72
10		80
11		88
12		96

Day 26

Fast Facts!

7 X 6 =42	*7 X 1 =7*	*7 X 5 =35*	*7 X 11 = 77*	*10 X 7 = 70*
7 X 4 =28	*7 X 8 =56*	*9 X 7 =63*	*7 X 8 = 56*	*2 X 7 = 14*
8 X 7 =56	*3 X 7 =21*	*6 X 7 =42*	*12 X 7 = 84*	*7 X 7 = 49*
5 X 7 =35	*7 X 7 =49*	*1 X 7 =7*	*7 X 3 = 21*	*7 X 9 = 63*

Multiplication Maze!

		1	2	3	4	5	6	7	8	9	10	
	1										10	**End!**
	2			6	8	10	12			18	20	
	3			9			18		24	27		
	4	4	8	12	16		24		32			
	5				20		30	35	40	45	50	
Start!	**6**	6			24			42				
	7	7	14	21	28			49				

Use Your Tools!

Makayla and Trey are planning to sign up for the school talent show...

8 boxes for Makayla + 8 boxes for Trey = 16 boxes

16 = 10 + 6

12 X 10 = 120   12 X 6 = 72

120 + 72 = 192

After the show, Makayla ate 2 boxes and Trey ate 4. How many total donuts did they eat together?

2 + 4 = 6

6 boxes X 12 donuts = 72

Their friends, Tina and Theresa, had best performance...

7 frogs X 12 bikes = 84

Day 27

Fast Facts!

8 X 1 = 8	*8 X 5 = 40*	*8 X 9 = 72*
8 X 2 = 16	*8 X 6 = 48*	*8 X 10 = 80*
8 X 3 = 24	*8 X 7 = 56*	*8 X 11 = 88*
8 X 4 = 32	*8 X 8 =64*	*8 X 12 = 96*

Flex 'Em!

A giraffe is going jogging ...

8 socks X 4 feet = 32 socks

Got that? OK- 4 giraffes are going jogging.

4 giraffes X 4 feet = 16 feet

16 feet X 8 socks =

16 = 10 + 6

10 X 8 = 80 6 X 8 = 48

80 + 48 = 128

Work It Out!

Jane loves giant chocolate chip cookies...

IN		OUT
4	5 orange slices	20
5		25
6		30
7		35
8		40

IN		OUT
4	6 orange slices	24
5		30
6		36
7		42
8		48

Build Your Skills!

Michael and Margot are building a couch fort in the living room...

4ft X 8ft = 32 square ft	5ft X 11ft = 55 square ft	5ft X 8ft = 40 square ft

Day 28

	X 1	X 2	X 3	X 4	X 5	X 6	X 7	X 8	X 9	X 10	X 11	X 12
5:	5	10	15	20	25	30	35	40	45	50	55	60
6:	6	12	18	24	30	36	42	48	54	60	66	72
7:	7	14	21	28	35	42	49	56	63	70	77	84
8:	8	16	24	32	40	48	56	64	72	80	88	96
9:	9	18	27	36	45	54	63	72	81	90	99	108

Work It Out!

X	7	8	9
0	0	0	0
1	7	8	9
2	14	16	18

X	8	9	10
4	32	36	40
5	40	45	50
6	48	54	60

X	10	11	12
6	60	66	72
7	70	77	84
8	80	88	96

Fast Facts!

8 X 6 =48	8 X 1 = 8	8 X 5 = 40	8 X 11 = 88	10 X 8 = 80
8 X 4 = 32	7 X 8 = 56	9 X 8 = 72	8 X 8 = 64	2 X 8 = 16
8 X 8 = 64	3 X 8 = 24	6 X 8 = 48	12 X 8 = 96	4 X 8 = 32
5 X 8 = 40	8 X 2 = 16	1 X 8 = 8	8 X 3 = 24	7 X 8 = 56

Day 29

Use Your Tools!

Stewart has requested a 8-tier strawberry birthday cake...

8 tiers X 6 strawberries = 48 strawberries

Stewart's mom has decided to decorate the cake with 8 sugar 8's on each of the 8 tiers. How many 8's will that be?

8 8's X 8 tiers = 64 8's

Fast Facts!

8 X 1 = 8	8 X 5 = 40	8 X 9 = 72
8 X 2 = 16	8 X 6 = 48	8 X 10 = 80
8 X 3 = 24	8 X 7 = 56	8 X 11 = 88
8 X 4 = 32	8 X 8 =64	8 X 12 = 96

Multiplication Maze!

		1	2	3	4	5	6	7	8	9	10	
	1		2									
	2		4	6	8	10	12		16	18	20	
Start!	**3**	3	6				18		24			
	4				16	20	24		32			
	5			15	20				40			
	6		12	18			36	42	48		60	**End!**
	7			21			42		56		70	
	8			24	32	40	48		64	72	80	
	9			27								

Day 30

Fast Facts!

8 X 6 = 48	*8 X 1 = 8*	*8 X 5 = 40*	*8 X 11 = 88*	*10 X 8 = 80*
8 X 4 = 32	*7 X 8 = 56*	*9 X 8 = 72*	*8 X 8 = 64*	*2 X 8 = 16*
8 X 8 = 64	*3 X 8 = 24*	*6 X 8 = 48*	*12 X 8 = 96*	*4 X 8 = 32*
5 X 8 = 40	*8 X 2 = 16*	*1 X 8 = 8*	*8 X 3 = 24*	*7 X 8 = 56*

Work It Out!

Tommy has an enormous button collection.

6 X 9 = 54	9 X 11 = 99	7 X 9= 63
9 X 3 = 27	9 X 2 = 18	9 X 12 = 108

Work It Out!

Bailey's parents have agreed to give her $8 ...

IN		OUT
2		16
3	$8 per	24
4		32
5		40
6		48

IN		OUT
2		18
3	$9 per	27
4		36
5		45
6		54

Use Your Tools!

Rhoda and Riley are building a castle out of twinkies!

1 tower = 9 layers X 4 twinkies per layer = 36 twinkies

6 towers X 36 twinkies per tower = ?

36 = 10 + 10 + 10 +6

6 X 10 = 60   6 X 10 = 60   6 X 10 = 60   6 X 6= 36

60 + 60 + 60 +36 = 216

Day 31

Build Your Skills!

	X 1	X 2	X 3	X 4	X 5	X 6	X 7	X 8	X 9	X 10	X 11	X 12
6:			18	24	30	36				60	66	72
7:	7			28	35			56			77	84
8:	8	16					56	64	72			96
9:	9	18	27	36	45	54	63	72	81	90	99	108

Work It Out!

X	12	11	10
9	108	99	90
8	96	88	80
7	84	77	70

X	9	8	7
4	36	32	28
3	27	24	21
2	18	16	14

X	10	9	8
7	70	63	56
6	60	54	48
5	50	45	40

Fast Facts!

9 X 1 = 9	*9 X 5 =45*	*9 X 9 = 81*
9 X 2 = 18	*9 X 6 = 54*	*9 X 10 = 90*
9 X 3 = 27	*9 X 7 = 63*	*9 X 11 = 99*
9 X 4 = 36	*9 X 8 = 72*	*9 X 12 = 108*

Use Your Tools!

Freddie has created a supply train out of several pairs of his father's shoes.

4 pairs of shoes = 4 X 2 = 8 shoes

8 shoes X 9 men = 72 men

What if Freddie adds his mothers shoes?

9 pairs of shoes = 9 X 2 = 18 shoes

18 shoes X 4 men = ?

18 = 10 + 8

4 X 10 = 40 4 X 8 = 32

40 + 32 = 72

Day 32

Build Your Skills!

	X 1	X 2	X 3	X 4	X 5	X 6	X 7	X 8	X 9	X 10	X 11	X 12
6:	6	12	18	24	30	36	42	48	54	60	66	72
7:	7	14	21	28	35	42	49	56	63	70	77	84
8:	8	16	24	32	40	48	56	64	72	80	88	96
9:	9	18	27	36	45	54	63	72	81	90	99	108
10:	10	20	30	40	50	60	70	80	90	100	110	120

Work It Out!

X	10	11	120
8	80	88	96
9	90	99	108
10	100	110	120

X	7	8	9
10	70	80	90
11	77	88	99
12	84	96	108

X	7	8	9
4	28	32	36
5	35	40	45
6	42	48	54

Multiplication Maze!

		1	2	3	4	5	6	7	8	9	10	
	3					15				27		
	4					20	24	28	32	36		
	5	5	10	15	20	25			40			
	6		12				36	42	48			
	7		14	21	28		42			63	70	**End!**
	8				32		48	56	64	72		
Start	9	9	18	27	36							

Fast Facts!

9 X 6 = 54	9 X 1 = 9	9 X 5 = 45	9 X 11 = 99	10 X 9 = 90
9 X 4 = 36	7 X 9 = 63	9 X 9 = 81	8 X 9 = 72	2 X 9 = 18
9 X 8 = 72	3 X 9 = 27	6 X 9 = 54	12 X 9 = 108	4 X 9 = 36
5 X 9 = 45	9 X 2 = 18	1 X 9 = 9	9 X 3 = 27	7 X 9 = 63

Day 33

Work It Out!

Derek is making tropical punch for his soccer team party

IN	Big	OUT
8	8 cups	64
9		72
10		80
11		88
12		96

IN	Small	OUT
8	9 cups	72
9		81
10		90
11		99
12		108

Work It Out!

10 is a great number to use when working with the distributive function.

3 X 16 = 16 = 10 + 6 3 X 10 = 30 3 X 6 = 18 30+ 18 = 48	**4 X 18 =** 18 = 10 + 8 4 X 10 = 40 4 X 8 = 32 40 + 32 = 72
2 X 13 = 13 = 10 + 3 2 X 10 = 20 2 X 3 = 6 20 + 6 = 26	**4 X 15 =** 15 = 10 + 5 4 X 10 = 40 4 X 5 = 20 40 + 20 = 60

Day 34

Fast Facts!

9 X 6 = 54	9 X 1 = 9	9 X 5 = 45	9 X 11 = 99	10 X 9 = 90
9 X 4 = 36	7 X 9 = 63	9 X 9 = 81	8 X 9 = 72	2 X 9 = 18
9 X 8 = 72	3 X 9 = 27	6 X 9 = 54	12 X 9 =108	4 X 9 = 36
5 X 9 = 45	9 X 2 = 18	1 X 9 = 9	9 X 3 = 27	7 X 9 = 63

Work It Out!

X	7	6	5
12	84	72	60
11	77	66	55
10	70	60	50

X	11	10	9
4	44	40	36
3	33	30	27
2	22	20	18

X	10	9	8
9	90	81	72
8	80	72	64
7	70	63	56

Use Your Tools!

James has dreamed himself into a real life video game....

5 mushrooms X 11 ft = 55 ft

On the next level, James has to collect rings ...

16 legs X 3 caterpillars = ?

16 = 10 + 6

3 X 10 = 30

3 X 6 = 18

30 + 18 = 48

Finally, James must hit each lady bug on the head 7 times...

7 hits X 12 lady bugs = 84 hits

Day 35

Build Your Skills!

	X 1	X 2	X 3	X 4	X 5	X 6	X 7	X 8	X 9	X 10	X 11	X 12
7:	7	14	21	28	35	42	49	56	63	70	77	84
8:	8	16	24	32	40	48	56	64	72	80	88	96
9:	9	18	27	36	45	54	63	72	81	90	99	108
10:	10	20	30	40	50	60	70	80	90	100	110	120
11:	11	22	33	44	55	66	77	88	99	110	121	132

Work It Out!

X	10	11	12
9	90	99	108
10	100	110	120
11	110	121	132

X	8	9	10
4	32	36	40
5	40	45	50
6	48	54	60

X	7	8	9
2	14	16	18
3	21	24	27
4	28	32	36

Fast Facts!

11 X 1 = 11	*11 X 5 = 55*	*11 X 9 = 99*
11 X 2 =22	*11 X 6 = 66*	*11 X 10 =110*
11 X 3 = 33	*11 X 7 = 77*	*11 X 11 = 121*
11 X 4 = 44	*11 X 8 = 88*	*11 X 12 = 132*

Multiplication Maze!

		1	2	3	4	5	6	7	8	9	10	
	5						30					
	6			18	24	30	36	42		54		
	7		14	21				49		63		
	8			24		40	48	56		72	80	
	9		18	27		45			72	81	90	
	10		20			50	60	70	80		100	
Start!	11	11	22			55					110	End!

Day 36

Fast Facts!

10 X 6 = 60	*10 X 1 = 10*	*10 X 5 = 50*	*10 X 11 = 110*	*10 X 10 = 100*
10 X 4 = 40	*7 X 10 = 70*	*9 X 10 = 90*	*8 X 10 = 80*	*2 X 10 = 20*
10 X 8 = 80	*3 X 10 = 30*	*6 X 10 = 60*	*12 X 10 = 120*	*4 X 10 = 40*
5 X 10 = 50	*10 X 2 = 20*	*1 X 10 = 10*	*10 X 3 = 30*	*7 X 10 = 70*

Flex 'Em!

Rory is having a "bandit" birthday party...

11 people X 4 items of disguise= 44 items

Work It Out!

Cassy has decided to make homemade cinnamon raisin bread...

IN		OUT
2	9 slices per loaf	18
3		27
4		36
5		45
6		54

IN		OUT
2	10 slices per loaf	20
3		30
4		40
5		50
6		60

Day 37

Fast Facts!

11 X 1 = 11	*11 X 5 = 55*	*11 X 9 = 99*
11 X 2 =22	*11 X 6 = 66*	*11 X 10 =110*
11 X 3 = 33	*11 X 7 = 77*	*11 X 11 = 121*
11 X 4 = 44	*11 X 8 = 88*	*11 X 12 = 132*

Work It Out!

Elliot is going to surprise his parents by constructing a giant ant farm ...

6ft X 10ft = **60 sq ft**	**11ft X 11ft =** **121 sq ft**	**7ft X 6ft=** **42 sq ft**
9ft X 10ft = **90 sq ft**	**8ft X 6ft =** **48 sq ft**	**5ft X 12ft =** **60 sq ft**

Multiplication Maze!

		3	4	5	6	7	8	9	10	11	12	
	3			15						33		
	4			20	24	28	32			44		
Start!	**5**	15	20	25			40			55		
	6						48			66	72	**End!**
	7		28	35	42	49	56			77		
	8		32							88		
	9		36			63	72	81	90	99		
	10		40	50	60	70		90				
	11		44					99				

Day 38

Fast Facts!

11 X 6 = 66	*11 X 1 = 11*	*11 X 5 = 55*	*11 X 11 = 121*	*11 X 10 = 110*
11 X 4 = 44	*7 X 11 = 77*	*9 X 11 = 99*	*8 X 11 = 88*	*2 X 11 = 22*
11 X 8 = 88	*3 X 11 = 33*	*6 X 11 = 66*	*12 X 11 = 132*	*4 X 11 = 44*
5 X 11 = 55	*11 X 2 = 22*	*1 X 11 = 11*	*11 X 3 = 33*	*7 X 11 = 77*

Build Your Skills!

	X 1	X 2	X 3	X 4	X 5	X 6	X 7	X 8	X 9	X 10	X 11	X 12
7:					35	42	49	56	63			84
8:				32	40	48	56	64			88	96
9:			27	36	45	54	63			90	99	108
10:		20	30	40	50	60			90	100	110	120
11:	11	22	33	44	55			88	99	110	121	132

Work It Out!

X	10	11	12
9	90	99	108
10	100	110	120
11	110	121	132

X	4	5	6
10	40	50	60
11	44	55	66
12	48	60	72

X	8	9	10
9	72	81	90
10	80	90	100
11	88	99	110

Use Your Tools!

Alecia has gotten a pogo-stick for her birthday...

Alecia- 9 ft X 10 jumps = 90 ft

Aaron- 7 ft X 10 jumps = 70 ft

Day 39

Build Your Skills

	X 1	**X 2**	**X 3**	**X 4**	**X 5**	**X 6**	**X 7**	**X 8**	**X 9**	**X 10**	**X 11**	**X 12**
8:			24	32	40	48				80	88	96
9:	9			36	45			72			99	108
10:	10	20					70	80	90			120
11:	11	22	33			66	77	88	99	110		
12:	12	24	36	48	60	72	84	96	108	120	132	144

Fast Facts!

12 X 1 = 12	*12 X 5 = 60*	*12 X 9 = 108*
12 X 2 =24	*12 X 6 = 72*	*12 X 10 = 120*
12 X 3 = 36	*12 X 7 = 84*	*12 X 11 = 132*
12 X 4 = 48	*12 X 8 = 96*	*12 X 12 = 144*

Use Your Tools!

Danny and DeShawn are playing hedgehog invaders...

6 X 12 = 72	9 X 12 = 108	7 X 12= 84
12 X 3 = 36	12 X 2 = 24	12 X 12 = 144

Work It Out!

X	12	11	10
12	144	132	120
11	132	121	110
10	120	110	100

X	12	11	10
4	48	44	40
3	36	33	30
2	24	22	20

X	12	11	10
9	108	99	90
8	96	88	80
7	84	77	70

Day 40

Fast Facts!

11 X 6 = 66	*11 X 1 = 11*	*11 X 5 = 55*	*11 X 11 = 121*	*11 X 10 = 110*
11 X 4 = 44	*7 X 11 = 77*	*9 X 11 = 99*	*8 X 11 = 88*	*2 X 11 =22*
11 X 8 = 88	*3 X 11 = 33*	*6 X 11 = 66*	*12 X 11 =132*	*4 X 11 =44*
5 X 11 = 55	*11 X 2 = 22*	*1 X 11 = 11*	*11 X 3 = 33*	*7 X 11 =77*

Work It Out!

Mariah is trying to calculate how much face-paint she needs...

IN		OUT
4	11 stars per face	44
5		55
6		66

IN		OUT
4	12 stars per face	48
5		60
6		72

Giant Multiplication Maze!

		1	2	3	4	5	6	7	8	9	10	
Start	0	0	0	0	0	0	0	0	0			
	1								8			
	2	2	4	6	8	10			16			
	3		6			15			24	27	30	
	4		8		16	20			32			
	5		10		20				40			
	6		12		24	30	36	42	48			
	7		14									
	8		16	24	32	40		56	64	72		
	9			27				63		81		
	10			30				70		90		
	11			33	44	55	66	77		99	110	End
	12		24	36	48					108		

Day 41

Fast Facts

12 X 1 = 12	*12 X 5 = 60*	*12 X 9 = 108*
12 X 2 =24	*12 X 6 = 72*	*12 X 10 = 120*
12 X 3 = 36	*12 X 7 = 84*	*12 X 11 = 132*
12 X 4 = 48	*12 X 8 = 96*	*12 X 12 = 144*

Work It Out!

Bernard is preparing the hot chocolate for his 4th grade class...

4 cups X 12 mm's = 48	9 cups X 7 mm's = 63	5 cups X 10 mm's= 50
12 cups X 3 mm's= 36	8 cups X 9 mm's = 72	11 cups X 11 mm = 121

Use Your Tools!

Reni and Rooster are next-door neighbours...

5 **tip-toes X 4 kids = 20 tip-toes**

How many stretches will be conducted if all 4 kids run the obstacle course?
22 stretches X 4 kids = ?

22= 10 + 12

4 X 10 = 40

4 X 12 = 48

40 + 48 = 88

Finally, how many swings will there be if Myra goes home but Maddy, Reni, and Rooster complete the course 1 more time?

11 swings X 3 kids = 33

Day 42

Fast Facts!

12 X 6 = 72	12 X 1 =12	12 X 5 = 60	12 X 11 = 132	12 X 10 = 120
12 X 4 = 48	7 X 12 = 84	9 X 12 = 108	8 X 12 = 96	2 X 12 =24
12 X 8 = 96	3 X 12 = 36	6 X 12 = 72	12 X 12 = 144	4 X 12 =48
5 X 12 = 60	12 X 2 = 24	1 X 12 = 12	12 X 3 = 36	7 X 12 =84

Work It Out!

Having had enough of Zorbo's nonsense, President Earnest World...

IN		OUT
8	Dial Set to 11	88
9		99
10		110
11		121
12		132

IN		OUT
8	Dial Set to 12	96
9		108
10		120
11		132
12		144

Build Your Skills!

X	10	11	12
10	100	110	120
11	110	121	132
12	120	132	144

X	7	8	9
6	42	48	54
7	49	56	63
8	56	64	72

X	10	11	12
9	90	99	108
10	100	110	120
11	110	121	132

Use Your Tools!

Did you know that bamboo can grow up to 15 inches per day?

10 shoots X 15 inches = 150 inches

What if she has 100 bamboo shoots? How many inches of bamboo will grow each day now?

100 shoots X 15 inches = 1500 inches

Day 43

Work It Out!

Zena has a small menagerie of animals...

6 X 6 = **36**	**9 X 9 =** **81**	**8 X 8=** **64**
7 X 7 = **49**	**11 X 11 =** **121**	**12 X 12 =** **144**

Fast Facts!

1 X 1 = 1	5 X 5 = 25	*9 X 9 = 81*
2 X 2 = 4	*6 X 6 = 36*	*10 X 10 = 100*
3 X 3 = 9	*7 X 7 = 49*	11 X 11 = 121
4 X 4 = 16	8 X 8 = 64	12 X 12 = 144

Giant Multiplication Maze!

		1	**2**	**3**	**4**	**5**	**6**	**7**	**8**	**9**	**10**	
	0											
	1				4	5	6	7				
Start!	**2**				8			14	16	18		
	3	3	6	9	12			21		27		
	4							28		36		
	5			15	20	25	30	35	40	45		
	6			18						54	60	
	7			21		35	42	49				
	8		16	24		40		56		72	80	**End!**
	9		18			45		63		81		
	10		20	30	40	50		70		90		
	11		22					77		99		
	12		24					84	96	108		

Day 44

Fast Facts!

1 X 100 = 100	5 X 100 = 500	9 X 100 = 900
2 X 100 = 200	6 X 100 = 600	10 X 100 = 1000
3 X 100 = 300	7 X 100 = 700	11 X 100 = 1100
4 X 100 = 400	8 X 100 = 800	12 X 100 = 1200

Work It Out!

X	5	6	7
5	25	30	35
6	30	36	42
7	35	42	49

X	10	11	12
10	100	110	120
11	110	121	132
12	120	132	144

X	7	8	9
7	49	56	63
8	56	64	72
9	63	72	81

Use Your Tools!

Zorbo has designed mech-suits for his squirrel army...

Gears= 6000 gears X 5000 squirrels =

30 and six zeros

30,000,000- that's 30 million!

Day 45

Fast Facts!

12 X 6 = 72	*12 X 1 = 12*	*12 X 5 = 60*	*12 X 11 = 132*	*12 X 10 = 120*
12 X 4 = 48	*7 X 12 = 84*	*9 X 12 = 108*	*8 X 12 = 96*	*2 X 12 =24*
12 X 8 = 96	*3 X 12 = 36*	*6 X 12 =72*	*12 X 12 =144*	*4 X 12 =48*
5 X 12 = 60	*12 X 2 = 24*	*1 X 12 =12*	*12 X 3 = 36*	*7 X 12 =84*

Multiplication Maze!

		3	4	5	6	7	8	9	10	11	12	
	6			30	36	42			60			
Start!	**7**	21	28	35					70	77	84	
	8		32			56	64	72	80		96	
	9		36	45	54	63			90		108	
	10							90	100		120	
	11						88	99			132	
	12				72	84	96				144	**End!**

Use Your Tools!

President World needs your help!

20,000 X 200 = 2 X 2 and six zeros

4,000,000

Made in the USA
Middletown, DE
28 June 2017